AF194428

EUROPE AND LATIN AMERICA

AN ANNUAL REVIEW OF EUROPEAN-LATIN AMERICAN RELATIONS

1980

Practical
ACTION
PUBLISHING

Latin America Bureau
Research and action on Latin America

Practical Action Publishing Ltd
25 Albert Street, Rugby, CV21 2SD, Warwickshire, UK
www.practicalactionpublishing.com

First published in 1980 by the Latin America Bureau
(Research and Action) Ltd,
1 Arnwell Street, London EC1R 1UL

The Latin America Bureau is an independent research and publishing
organisation. It works to broaden public understanding of issues of human
rights and social and economic justice in Latin America and the Caribbean.

Reprinted by Practical Action Publishing
Rugby, Warwickshire UK

ISBN0 906156 09 2
ISBN13: 9780906156094
ISBN Library Ebook: 9781909013636
Book DOI: http://dx.doi.org/10.3362/9781909013636

A Bolivar Design
Typeset by the Russell Press Ltd, Nottingham

Since 1974, Practical Action Publishing has published and disseminated books and
information in support of international development work throughout the world.
Practical Action Publishing is a trading name of Practical Action Publishing Ltd
(Company Reg. No. 1159018), the wholly owned publishing company of Practical
Action. Practical Action Publishing trades only in support of its parent charity
objectives and any profits are covenanted back to Practical Action (Charity Reg.
No. 247257, Group VAT Registration No. 880 9924 76).

The manufacturer's authorised representative in the EU for product safety is
Lightning Source France, 1 Av. Johannes Gutenberg, 78310 Maurepas, France.
compliance@lightningsource.fr

CONTENTS

Contributors   4

Preface   5

'Business as Usual': Britain's Tory Government
and Latin America   6
Colin Henfrey and Liz Nash

The European Labour Movement's Latin American
Dilemma   26
Don Thomson

European-Latin American Relations: A Latin
American View   38
Alberto Orlandi

European Direct Investment and the Brazilian
Economic Model   45
Peter-Uwe Schliemann

Europe and Latin America: The Nuclear
Connection   61
Jean Carriere

Appendices   73
Notes
Appendix 1 — Trade   75
Appendix 2 — Investment   75
Appendix 3 — Aid   75
Appendix 4 — Arms Sales   76

CONTRIBUTORS

Jean Carriere is a member of staff of the Centro de Estudios y Documentacion Latinoamericanos (CEDLA) in Amsterdam.

Colin Henfrey is lecturer in sociology at the Department of Sociology and Centre for Latin American Studies, University of Liverpool, and is a member of the Labour Party NEC's Sub-Committee on Latin America.

Liz Nash works as a researcher on Latin America in the Labour Party's International Department.

Alberto Orlandi is on the staff of the Division of International Trade and Development of the United Nations Economic Commission for Latin America (ECLA) in Santiago, Chile.

Peter-Uwe Schliemann is a research student in the Department of International Business at the London Business School.

Don Thomson is a writer on trade union internationalism and author of *Where Were You Brother.*

PREFACE

In 1978 the Latin America Bureau published the first issue of *Britain and Latin America,* an annual review of British-Latin American relations which aimed to examine critically Britain's role in the region. In the process of compiling this and the following year's review the increasing interest and involvement of other European, especially EEC, countries in Latin America became apparent, as did the importance of the European context in influencing Britain's relations with the subcontinent. As a result, the 1979 annual review included aspects of European involvement in the region. This year we have decided to go a step further and broaden the scope of the entire review, and to change its name to *Europe and Latin America.*

Our basic aim, however, remains the same. The interrelated problems of underdevelopment, poverty, dictatorship and repression still persist in Latin America. Many Latin American governments pursue economic policies which deepen social inequalities and conflict and which are frequently implemented through the supression of civil and political rights. The conduct of European governments and companies towards Latin America often implicitly supports dictatorial regimes and actually reinforces rather than helps solve the causes of underdevelopment. We believe that European involvement in Latin America should be the subject of critical debate with a view to promoting a more equitable distribution of wealth and respect for human rights in the region.

This first review of European-Latin American relations examines the European connection in the important areas of foreign investment, nuclear development and labour struggles in Latin America and presents a Latin American argument for a more positive and cooperative approach by Europe in its economic relations with the region. It also takes a hard look at the self-interest and contradictions behind the British Conservative government's policy towards Latin America.

Latin America Bureau
May 1980

'BUSINESS AS USUAL': BRITAIN'S TORY GOVERNMENT AND LATIN AMERICA
COLIN HENFREY AND LIZ NASH

British governments have traditionally placed relations with Latin America low on their list of priorities. But since coming to power in May 1979, the Conservatives have already adopted an approach quite distinct from that of their Labour predecessors. In particular, they have moved rapidly to 'normalise' relations with Latin American military regimes, notably Chile and Argentina, with the aim of maximising opportunities for British business in the continent.

It is hardly surprising that 'business as usual', even with such notorious regimes, should be the first consideration of so right-wing a government. Indeed in the present political climate of resurgent cold war sentiments, there is clearly some British sympathy for building bridges with the generals who proclaim themselves the saviours of 'Western and Christian civilisation' against 'Communist subversion' in Latin America.

However, it is also widely known that their regimes are among the most brutal and anti-democratic in modern history. In view of this, and the Carter administration's injection of human rights considerations into its foreign policy, the Conservatives have felt obliged to produce some more than merely commercial rationalisation of their position. The result has been a welter of contradictory statements, with which we deal first, on how their rapprochement with the dictators relates to the issues of human rights and democracy in Latin America. On the one hand they deny that such issues are relevant to diplomatic or economic relations: these are technical matters, and do not imply endorsement of the regimes in question. On the other hand the Conservatives suggest that these closer relations may help to improve human rights conditions. Yet in practice it is evident that their real effect is one of endorsement of the status quo. Moreover, the objective possibility of such improvements in human rights is limited precisely by the economic policies which the dictators are pursuing, with the Conservatives' explicit approval.

But aside from questions of social justice, how rational is this approval, even in economic terms? Next, we discuss the equally to have a representative in each country so that at least you have somebody through whom to talk, and to talk at a high level; that is one of the ways that we can secure some influence.'

Moreover, Nicholas Ridley added, having full diplomatic relations also favoured the prospects of democracy, on which genuine respect for human rights was necessarily dependent. He was somewhat uncertain about these prospects, referring acrobatically to the 'faltering but steady (sic) progress towards the re-establishment of democratic regimes' in Latin America. But the professed commitment was clear: 'all we can do on the political front will be directed to ensuring that those countries which are democracies remain so, and trying to encourage those that aren't to become so.'

What he singularly failed to appreciate was that the laissez-faire policies of Latin American regimes may be objectively at odds with the prospects for their redemocratisation. Indeed he saw no relationship between these factors, nor any possibility that the strengthening of British links would encourage repressive and dictatorial rather then democratic tendencies.

So much for the government's stated position. How well is it borne out in practice, first with regard to human rights? Officially, as frequently reiterated by Nicholas Ridley, the sending of an ambassador does not imply approval of a country's record on human rights, nor any suggestion that is has improved. In reality this turns out to be a hollow argument of convenience. The renewal of full diplomatic relations has clearly had such implications of approval, and both the Videla and Pinochet juntas have been quick to exploit them. For instance, Nicholas Ridley in his CIIR talk deplored Argentina's human rights record; yet he also suggested that it was understandable in the light of 'the exact nature of what is going on', namely 'the strength of the terrorist opposition.' He then added: 'Thank goodness, I hope and pray, that things are now improving a little bit'.

In addition to the muddled equation of the hope for improvement with actual improvement, this is in fact a clear attempt not only to suggest improvement, but to justify renewed full relations on the very grounds of human rights which the same speaker had previously ruled out as a consideration. So on the one hand the government professes a commitment to human rights. On the other it denies their relevance to such 'technical' questions as full recognition; yet in the context of such recognition it also compulsively suggests that they are no longer a serious problem. They thereby provide an endorsement which is not only groundless, but by their own logic unnecessary and gratuitous.

These contradictions are not just verbal. They are equally evident in government actions, beginning with the long-expected closure of the Latin American refugee programme, announced on 29 October 1979. Under this scheme, introduced following the Chilean coup of 1973, over 3000 refugees had entered Britain, all but a handful under the Labour government. In justifying the closure, Home Secretary William Whitelaw said that the number of such refugees arriving in Britain was diminishing. He also referred to the need for savings in the light of new commitments to Vietnamese refugees. Also, in a recent letter to a constituent, Nicholas Ridley has suggested that the original decision to establish a special programme was partisan and unnecessary. These three points deserve some investigation.

The reference to diminishing numbers was quite simply sleight of hand. Far from indicating a dimunution of the refugee problem, the declining number of those arriving was actually a consequence of government actions in deliberately running the programme down. Since coming to power the Conservatives had refused the majority of an *increasing* number of applications to come to Britain. According to Home Office statistics, between June and October 1979 only 21 applications were accepted and as many as 67 rejected. In July the number of applications awaiting decisions (173) was the highest since the peak level of September 1977. And in September 1979 there were still more applications pending (161) than there had been a year earlier (107), despite the fact that many would-be applicants were inevitably deterred from applying by the six month delay in getting a reply from the Home Office. The UNHCR representative in Brazil said in a letter to the Joint Working Group for Refugees from Latin America written on 31 October 1979, that he was no longer encouraging refugees to apply to Britain because the ensuing delay was often longer than the length of time refugees were allowed to stay within the country under UNHCR mandate.

As to the second official reason for the closure of the programme, the costs, in support of the Joint Working Group's programme for reception and settlement, amounted only to £126,000 per year. That the programme could be run so cheaply, relative to the large numbers involved, was because most of the work was done by human rights activists and members of the labour movement. To imply that the programme was competing with that for the Vietnamese refugees was a quite gratuitous attempt, under the guise of charity, to range the interests of one unfortunate refugee group against another's.

Most inconsistent of all, however, were the comments on the programme's original status, with doubt being cast on the necessity of a special programme in the first place. On the one hand William Whitelaw was to write to Labour Party General Secretary Ron Hayward on 17 January 1980:

'We have, of course been one of the leading countries in accepting refugees from Latin America, and it was a Conservative Home Secretary who introduced the Latin American refugee programme in October 1973.'

But just three days earlier, Nicholas Ridley had written in a letter to a constituent:

'I can tell you that there is no need, and never was, for a special programme . . . The intention of a special programme was a public relations exercise of the last government which is better buried.' (Letter to Mr Martin Davis, 14 January 1980).

This bizarre discrepancy between two ministers in the same government reveals the Janus face of the Conservative position. Apart from the factual inconsistency over who introduced the programme, William Whitelaw professes his party's concern for the Latin American refugee problem, but decides to terminate the programme. Nicholas Ridley, on the other hand, in one of his many unguarded moments, admits the cynically partisan nature of this Conservative decision.

For this partisanship, masquerading as liberalism and practicality, was clearly the essence of the matter. The Conservatives' fundamental objection to the special programme was ideological. It created an uncomfortable bone of contention with Latin American regimes whose 'liberalism' they so approved of, and with which they wished to restore their 'normal' diplomatic and business relations. How could Britain re-establish such relations with Latin America's dictators when the existence of the special programme was a constant reminder of these regimes' repressive nature? Helping refugees was, after all, a concrete way in which most European governments demonstrated their concern for human rights. In scrapping the programme, the Conservatives showed that 'normalising' relations with Latin America's dictators mattered more to them than being out of line with Britain's major European partners, and the United States and Canada, all of whom retain special programmes for Latin American refugees. Moreover, in the light of the government's claims, the decision was doubly ironic. The official statment on the return of the ambassador to Chile claimed quite categorically: 'When it comes to human rights, this Government prefers actions to words.' Yet its major action on human rights has been to abolish this one sure means of providing for some of the thousands of victims of continuing human rights violations.

'Business as usual', despite conflicting human rights considerations, was also the reason for returning the ambassadors to both Argentina and Chile. The decision on Argentina was announced in July 1979. The ambassador had been withdrawn in January 1976, not on human rights grounds, but after a shot was fired across the bows of a British survey ship by the Argentinian navy near the Falkland Islands. This dispute, as Nicholas Ridley admitted, remains unsettled. But, following the military coup in Argentina in March 1976, the decision to maintain diplomatic relations at a reduced level was reinforced by the appalling human rights violations under the Videla regime. Thus the renewal of full relations was immediately seen as a suggestion that the human rights situation had improved — an implication which Nicholas Ridley came close to conveying, as already shown, and which the Argentinians themselves have made explicit. Nevertheless, the Conservatives' decision aroused little opposition. This was largely because of the unfamiliarity of the Argentinian situation to most of the British labour movement.

Returning the ambassador to Chile, however, was more difficult to handle. Unlike Videla's, the Pinochet coup had suppressed a fairly European style labour movement and brought to an end an experiment in democratic socialism which many people in Britain viewed with sympathy and solidarity. Also two Britons, Sheila Cassidy and William Beausire, were victims of the junta's repression. These factors were familiar to and much emphasised by members of the labour movement in Britain. The delaying of the decision to return the ambassador to Chile until 17 January 1980 was indicative of the opposition which the Conservatives sensed on the issue.

Hence too the backroom quality of negotiations on the matter, such as the meeting between Chile's foreign minister Hernan

Cubillos and Lord Carrington on 4 September 1979. This visit, though shrouded in secrecy, was clearly a preliminary to restoring full diplomatic relations; the shower of protests which it provoked from the labour movement, so near to the 11 September anniversary of the coup, doubtless influenced the government to postpone the decision. Meanwhile, however, the ground for this was being prepared, though not without elaborate contortions. Lord Carrington had expressed the Conservative position on ambassadorial relations in a letter to Ron Hayward, General Secretary of the Labour Party, on 29 August 1979, and he tried to sidestep the implications of this position by imputing it to Labour as well. He wrote:

'I should, however, like to make the general point about diplomatic representation — and I think it is common ground between our parties — that whatever the country concerned, the fact of having ambassadors does not in any way constitute approval or support by us for a particular regime or its policies.'

In fact the ambassador's withdrawal had been occasioned precisely by the nature of the Chilean regime and its actions. It was following the imprisonment and torture of Dr Sheila Cassidy in 1975 that the Labour government had taken this step. Moreover, at the time it had the support of the other parties, the Conservatives included. Their subsequent reluctance to acknowledge this background, when they returned the ambassador — the better to argue that this was simply the 'normalisation' of an anomaly — was to lead to the most embarassing of their contradictions over Latin America, which erupted into a minor scandal.

On 30 August 1979 Nicholas Ridley told a delegation from the Chile Committee for Human Rights that Labour had withdrawn the ambassador for the essentially political reason that a right-wing government had taken over from a left-wing one. Later, at the CIIR meeting, he stated that the decision to restore the ambassador was taken, 'because we believe it to be right to have ambassadorial representation wherever possible with states we recognise . . . To suggest that it represents a condonation of the Chilean government record on human rights is a misrepresentation.'

However, in obscuring the original reason for the ambassador's withdrawal he had already taken a clear step towards whitewashing the Chilean junta. The decision to restore full diplomatic relations was a virtual endorsement of Pinochet, despite the government's disclaimers, as a *Times* editorial indicated on 18 January 1980:

'The decision by a Conservative government to send an ambassador once again suggests either that the Conservatives do not take such a serious view of the behaviour of the armed forces in Chile or else that they consider there has been a significant improvement in human rights there. This, at least, is the way that it will be interpreted both in Chile and elsewhere, and in either case it will give considerable encouragement to President Pinochet and his regime.'

For the fact is that no satisfaction has been given on the original issue. The Chileans have never brought to justice those responsible for Sheila Cassidy's torture nor made any commitment to do so. Hence, with the decision to return the ambassador to Chile, an evident reluctance to admit that Dr Cassidy had been tortured at all began to pervade Foreign Office thinking. This became clear when Nicholas Ridley spoke of the grudging apology which he had received from the Chilean junta for the treatment Dr Cassidy *may* have received (our emphasis). Then, in early February, soon after the ambassador's return, he told a Chile Solidarity Campaign delegation led by Judith Hart that Sheila Cassidy might have been mistaken about her treatment.

The Foreign Office tried to counter the storm of protest this aroused, by saying later that it was impossible to decide between the junta's and Dr Cassidy's version of events. But as the shadow Foreign Secretary Peter Shore pointed out, even this amounted to a revision of the whole background to the withdrawal of the ambassador in the first place. 'Nobody has previously questioned the veracity of Dr Sheila Cassidy's account of what happened to her or the detailed statement she made to the Foreign Office on her return to London,' he said, in a statement on 8 February 1980. This was later corroborated when the Foreign Office finally backtracked completely on the issue, admitting that Dr Cassidy's testimony was indeed indisputable, but adding: 'we have been unable to obtain the Chilean government's acceptance of it.'

Two conclusions can be drawn from this sorry story. First, it is once more symptomatic of how the renewal of 'normal' relations does indeed entail an effective endorsement of dictatorial repression. And secondly, the underlying economic significance of this 'normalisation' was soon apparent. On 14 January 1980 the government revealed that the Export Credit Guarantees Department had underpinned the payment and funding of two separate five million dollar lines of credit from the London finance houses Lazard Brothers and NM Rothschild, to the Bank of Chile. These were intended to help finance British capital goods and service contracts placed in Britain by Chilean buyers. Lord Carrington said that this decision was taken on purely commercial grounds. Here at least he was frank, since this is clearly the paramount principle of Conservative policy towards Latin America.

With international opinion so widely ranged against the junta for its persistent human rights violations, the Conservatives' de facto endorsement of it has been demonstrated in other ways no less incompetent and contradictory. The continuing deterioration of Chilean human rights conditions was meticulously described in the UN Special Rapporteur's report of November 1979. In December Britain, along with 93 other countries, supported a resolution expressing deep concern at the report's findings, which were as follows: harassment and torture were occuring more frequently in Chile; killings by armed forces and security services continued; disappearances were not being investigated; persecution of trade unionists was increasing, and legal protection for them decreasing; exiles were not allowed to return, despite the 'amnesty'; and finally, freedom of association and the right of assembly were denied.

Yet despite Britain's backing of this report, Nicholas Ridley as Minister of State has systematically and publicly denied almost every one of the points which it mentions, in arguing against all the evidence and the stated position of his government, that human rights in Chile have improved. In March a Labour Party delegation of NEC members and front bench spokesmen confronted the Foreign Secretary Lord Carrington with this discrepancy. His answer was a mystifying rigmarole to the effect that the human rights situation was 'static . . . (it) was certainly not getting any worse, nor indeed was there a great deal of improvement . . . the rate of improvement had slowed down.' And so on. Finally, Ted Rowlands, former Labour minister with responsibility for Latin America, read to the Foreign Secretary the relevant passages of the UN report. At this point Lord Carrington dismissed the problem. There would, he said, have to remain a difference of opinion on the matter.

The contradictions which run consistently through these confused events are as follows. Whilst the Conservatives' commercial motives are in practice incompatible with human rights considerations, they nevertheless still genuflect to a hollow concern for human rights. They have two ways to try to reconcile these positions. One is to deny that such matters as restoring the ambassador are either influenced by human rights or have any implications for them. The other way is to suggest that human rights are now improving, and were perhaps never as bad as suggested. Sometimes they use the former argument, sometimes they prefer the latter, despite their being at odds with each other. One thing, though, they have in common: all the evidence indicates that each is palpably dishonest.

Both will no doubt continue to be used, particularly in apology for the final stage of 'normalisation': it can only be a matter of time before the Conservatives announce the resumption of arms sales to the Chilean junta.

The Free Market and the Prospects for Democracy in Latin America

Conservatives acknowledge that they are seeking closer links with Latin American regimes to further Britain's commercial interests. But this is reinforced by an ideological sympathy for the laissez-faire, free market economic policies which some of these regimes are pursuing. It is this sympathy which has led to the contradictions in the Conservative position: for authoritarian regimes and violations of human rights are not just aberrations, as Conservative reasoning implies. On the contrary, they are necessary consequences of policies which acutely disadvantage the majority of the population.

Conservatives argue that these policies will lead to economic growth; and that this in turn will facilitate the restoration of democracy. Recent experience, however, suggests the opposite: that free market liberalism is a recipe not for growth, but for economic crisis and industrial collapse in Latin America. Further, the social consequences of liberal economic policies are so harsh that they have proved to be incompatible with political democracy. Only in Brazil has marked growth occurred, not through economic liberalism but state intervention. Moreover, the dependence of even this growth on deepening social inequality has necessitated the same authoritarianism as the less successful economic liberalism of the juntas in Argentina and Chile. Since Nicholas Ridley particularly stressed what he sees as the prospects of these three countries, they are worth examining more closely.

Brazil's growth is undeniable, but based on distinctive factors. The most marked of these is the traditionally high degree of state intervention in the economy, particularly in manufacturing. Following the 1964 coup, this intervention was increased, with the state becoming a major determinant of economic planning. Key sectors of the economy are owned by the state, and its fiscal and monetary policies have substantial state involvement. Above all the state maintains a close control of wages, trades unions and labour relations. The continuing reluctance to relax this control, despite the increasing resistance of labour, is an indication of how vital it remains to the Brazilian regime.

Where the Brazilians have been 'liberal' is with foreign investment and social welfare. Generous terms have been given to foreign investors to attract their capital to Brazil, causing medium and small-sized national firms to collapse in large numbers; and proportionate public spending on items like health and education has been slashed.

As in laissez-faire Argentina and Chile, it is only capital, not labour, which is given a relatively free rein. What the Brazilian experience shows is that profitable free enterprise, particularly in manufacturing, is not in conflict with state intervention but dependent on it. In Latin America industrial progress has traditionally depended on the state sector to provide it with subsidised inputs like steel and fuel, an appropriate and reliable infrastructure, and a stable level of consumer demand, as well as the control of labour. The public sector is far from being the enemy of the private one, as Conservative demonology suggests, and key sectors of the Latin American right accept this. Many of Brazil's most successful ventures have been based on the partnership of state with international private capital.

In Argentina too, many industrialists have long since favoured state intervention as the basis of planned economic growth. This has its origins in the armed forces, where it was thought that self-sufficiency in basic industrial production was vital to national defence. Indeed many of Argentina's heavy industries are military installations, and thus state-owned. Following Videla's seizure of power in 1976, this current of thought was represented by planning minister Ramon Diaz Bessone, who put forward an ambitious 'national project' for comprehensive state control over economic and political life. Beginning with 'national reconstruction', this plan concluded with the founding of a 'new' – in effect a corporatist and military-dominated – republic. But in 1977, before this vision could be tested in practice, Bessone and his programme were replaced by the current, laissez-faire programme. Argentina, after all, despite its high level of industrial development, mainly lives off agricultural exports. Those involved – the big landowners and banking and import-export sectors – have long been powerful bastions of Argentinian economic liberalism. They provide the backing for the laissez-faire policies now adopted by Videla and administered by the economics minister, old-Etonian, landowner and financier, José Martinez de Hoz.

In Chile there was no such equivocation in the wake of the 1973 coup. Friedman-style free market policies were adopted quickly and ruthlessly. Pinochet's junta had deep political and ideological as well as economic reasons for curtailing the role of the Chilean state, since the Popular Unity had based its strategy on turning its powerful leverage on the Chilean economy in a more socialist direction.

There is, however, one area of state activity which has been increased even by the most extreme laissez-faire regimes: and this, of course, is the machinery of repression, especially concerning labour relations. In Argentina and Chile such controls are even more rigid than in Brazil, since in both these cases strong labour movements were better prepared to mount a resistance to the negative social consequences of liberal economic policies.

What are the characteristics of these policies? Who benefits? And who pays?

To summarise the measures taken: military rulers in Argentina and Chile have virtually abolished protective tariffs, withdrawn state support for industry, demolished welfare legislation, freed prices and sold off public companies to the private sector at knock-down prices. In each case the results have been disastrous, not only for industry but also for middle class consumers.

In Chile Pinochet's 'shock treatment', inspired by Milton Friedman as a necessary 'temporary disruption' to restructure the economy on laissez-faire lines, has plunged the country into its worst depression since 1930. Both unemployment and inflation reached record levels; whilst the latter has now fallen, the former seems permanent. Industrial investment is stagnant and official concern is being expressed at the failure of businessmen to 'rise to the challenge of increased competition'. Resources have been drastically concentrated: a recent study by a Chilean economist shows that six powerful economic 'clans' now control two thirds of the country's assets. Even the World Bank believes the result of all this is 'great material sacrifice on the part of the vast majority of Chilean citizens'.

The picture is similar in Argentina, where the bracing economic climate has brought the number of bankruptcies to an all time record. Industrialists' organisations in both countries are now openly critical of the laissez-faire policies so relentlessly pursued by the junta.

In the face of this generalised discontent, from employers and middle classes as well as the labour movement, it is hardly surprising that these two regimes show few signs of even the limited political relaxation promised. This is restricted to what Pinochet has called 'authoritarian democracy', with a vague and protracted timetable for renewing a measure of civilian participation, while maintaining military domination. Proposed constitutional measures include a ban on left-wing political parties, severe restrictions on trade unions, and the right of the military to veto government decisions.

Such is the 'faltering but steady progress' towards redemocratisation which Nicholas Ridley has detected. In Brazil sections of industry and a greatly expanded working class are now actively demanding change, but the government's elaborate stalling shows that, even where growth has been achieved, steps towards redemocratisation threaten the regime's continuation in its present form. Moves towards democracy are simply irreconcilable with statist or laissez-faire programmes which give overwhelming priority to the interests of banking and finance capital, the multinational corporations and big agricultural exporters and producers, at the expense of national industry, small business and the working classes, not to mention growing numbers of the unemployed and rural poor.

In the case of the laissez-faire regimes which Nicholas Ridley explicitly favours, there is little evidence, past or present, for even his economic arguments for closer ties. The beneficiaries of this laissez-faire — financiers and big landowners — are precisely those sectors which have proved historically the least able to generate self-sustaining growth in Latin America. Even since 1930, their pursuit of liberal economic policies in countries like Argentina has resulted in spectacular stagnation and decline. On the other hand, even where growth has resulted from policies favouring equally narrow interests, democracy seems little closer.

It may be, as Nicholas Ridley pleads, that the reason for Conservative involvement with the dictatorial status quo is not just the hope of short-term profits, but genuine ignorance of the region. But neither provides a very sound basis for developing good relations with Latin America in the future.

Towards an Alternative Policy: The Importance of the Labour Movement

As noted in last year's LAB Review, the main non-governmental influence on British policy towards Latin America is the Canning House consortium. Comprising businessmen, former Foreign Office staff and highly Conservative academics, it is geared to defending the status quo. Those involved, including organisations like the British-Chilean Council, are closely linked to the Latin American embassies in London. On the whole they are simply mouthpieces within the British ruling class for Latin American military regimes.

As such they have a quite unwarranted legitimacy in this country. For instance, on 4 June 1979, Viscount Montgomery, a leading member of Canning House and of the British-Chilean Council, wrote a sharp attack in the *Guardian* on the Labour government's policies towards Latin America. It was an unashamed apology for the military regimes in the region, and urged an immediate rapprochement with them. It seemed at the time to represent only Conservatism's lunatic fringe; but Conservative policy has since followed the recommendations of Viscount Mongomery remarkably closely.

It is worth noting that under US legislation groups like the British-Chilean Council would be bound to declare their interests and connections with military dictatorships. Pressure for such legislation in Britain should be part of any attempt to develop a more progressive policy towards Latin America. As it is, these groups' respectable facades in institutions like Canning House protect them from public scrutiny, and lend their reactionary views a spurious air of objectivity.

The deeper problem is that, given the British government machinery's admitted ignorance of Latin America, any views purporting to be 'expert' acquire an exaggerated air of truth. Clearly, in these circumstances, alternative mechanisms are needed, both to formulate and to implement policies to counter the minority interests represented in current Conservative thinking.

Nor is this just a matter of providing 'alternative information'. There are in Britain many progressive academics and journalists who work on Latin America, who can and do counter the orthodoxy of the Foreign Office and the propaganda from Canning House. What needs to be asked is: by whom is this propaganda supplied, and to whom is it so successfully directed? What gives right-wing views their weight is the strength of the business interests behind them, and the sympathy which they command in the higher ranks of the Conservative Party. What is therefore needed is not just a channel for proposing different policies, but a means of ensuring their adoption and their implementation by future governments.

The only potential basis for this change of direction is the labour movement. It alone can provide a counterweight to the business support for the status quo. There already exists in the Labour Party, through a sub-committee of its National Executive, a channel whereby information from Latin American specialists and the views of concerned trade unionists and the solidarity campaigns can contribute to policy formation. But two things remain to be developed. Firstly, the means of ensuring that a Labour government, once elected, will carry out the Party's policy; and secondly, a greater awareness of the issues among Labour Party members, together with their fuller involvement in the policy-making process. The first of these questions is currently under vigorous discussion in the Labour Party. As to the second, plans are being made for a party conference on foreign policy, designed precisely to deepen the involvement of party members in policy-making, and also to bring their attention more to international issues.

What emphasis might these new policies have once the basis for them is established? There seem to be at least three areas in which the positive – if limited – positions of the previous Labour government could be developed a great deal further.

With a serious commitment to human rights, concrete measures should be taken firstly to damage military dictatorships both economically and diplomatically; and secondly, to help their victims. The first would entail economic and political sanctions of various kinds on aid, trade, investment and financial loans. The second, in providing refuge for those who are fleeing from repression, is not only a concrete demonstration of genuine support for human rights, it is also an effective slap in the face to such dictatorial regimes, which spend much of their time in culling abroad the approval which they lack at home.

Thirdly, measures should be taken to aid and encourage the resistance within such Latin American countries. This means not just humanitarian aid to non-state organisations and charities but also the mobilisation, from suitable sources in Britain, of financial support for progressive political parties and popular movements in Latin America. The actual sums raised need not be crucial. What really matters is the impact of such mobilisation on awareness in the British labour movement, its demonstration of solidarity to the Latin American peoples concerned, and the warning it offers to their oppressors. Organisationally, this will depend on seeking out and identifying such democratic, progressive and socialist forces in Latin America; and on strengthening links between them and the British labour movement.

At grass roots level there is no lack of potential support for these connections. Ad hoc appeals for support or help made by Latin American trade unions and parties to sections of the labour movement have already prompted effective solidarity actions. Among many examples, Merseyside portworkers and seamen who had contact with their Chilean counterparts, and learnt of their repression by the junta, refused to handle cargo or man any vessels bound for Chile, despite the obvious problems involved in an area of declining employment. Such grass roots solidarity actions, often against the grain of bread and butter considerations, have been the main force behind the boycotts of Chilean trade at a higher level, by international trade union bodies.

Pressure from such grass roots sources was also a major influence on progressive decisions taken by the last Labour government, particularly over Chile, but also towards other countries suffering from dictatorship. For instance, something of a breakthrough occurred in international solidarity, when Bolivian miners appealed to the National Union of Mineworkers here to urge the British government to withold a loan negotiated with the Bolivian state mining corporation; this was in view of the Bolivian government's violations of trade union rights. Not only was this appeal successful, but the actions of moderate NUM executive members in visiting Bolivia, and Chile, and speaking about their experiences to meetings of other British workers, attracted unprecedented attention to what in Bolivia's case had been a relatively unknown country. Similarly, the effective response of the Iron and Steel Trades Confederation to appeals from the Argentinian metalworkers drew attention to the otherwise neglected atrocities going on under Videla.

International trade union and political bodies like the International Confederation of Free Trade Unions or the Socialist International, are also potentially important. Though often criticised as bureaucratic and ineffectual, they should not be underestimated. Full use should be made of their resources and contacts, as well as the influence which they wield, in developing policies which are likely to be more effective if pursued multilaterally. The Socialist International, to which the Labour Party belongs, is giving increasing attention to Latin America, and a growing number of progressive Latin American parties are looking to it for support. The fact that wholehearted support was given to the Nicaraguan Sandinistas by the Socialist International and many of its European members, including the British Labour Party, probably helped them to come to power and develop the degree of strength which they have today. Such support is especially important to small and progressive governments and parties in Central America and the Caribbean, as a counterweight to the intense US resistance to change in these regions. Especially in the case of former British colonies like Jamaica and revolutionary Grenada, the labour movement has an unfulfilled historical task of developing new ties of solidarity.

At the same time efforts need to be made to relate these international issues to domestic ones. Though easily exaggerated, the monetarist analogies and links between Thatcher's Britain and Pinochet's Chile afford a unique opportunity for highlighting Latin American issues. Evidence of this has been provided by a recent trade union conference, organised by Northampton Labour Party and the Chile Solidarity Campaign, on the question: 'Can monetarism work without dictatorship?' A similar conference is now being planned at a national level. The nub of both situations, after all, however different the mechanisms, is both governments' determination to reduce the levels of real wages by curbing the strength of the labour movement.

Regarding the effects for British workers of closer economic ties with such countries, Conservative policy is premised on the desirability of moving capital out of Britain, to countries where low wages and high profits are assured by dictatorial regimes. But it is precisely this exodus of capital which is ravaging areas like Merseyside with unemployment and industrial collapse. The implications are self-evident. Far from any conflict of interests between a 'labour aristocracy' and impoverished neo-colonial labour, the repression of workers like those in Chile and Argentina means unemployment for increasing numbers here in Britain.

The scope for mobilising the labour movement on such simultaneously domestic and international issues is obvious. And evidence already shows that neither exhortations nor appeals to self-interest are necessary. A sense of the international community of workers remains to this day a living element of the labour movement. What is still needed is some means of helping it effectively to counter the mechanisms of international capital ranged against it. For instance, the mobility of capital could be countered by a widespread campaign against its export, particularly to countries with repressive labour laws. With grass roots trade union and Labour Party participation, such campaigns could be mounted in the future.

However, the present political climate by no means rules out more immediate tasks. Having gone so far in the rapprochement with Chile's junta, the Conservatives are now clearly contemplating a renewal of the arms trade with Chile. Only the labour movement can offer effective resistance to such moves; but this is only possible if the necessary information is provided and pressure mobilised.

In addition, the government should still be pressed to continue to provide refuge to Latin Americans fleeing from repression, in line with its formal commitment to human rights. And given Nicholas Ridley's assurance that ambassadors will act on these questions, the labour movement and Labour MPs should be asking: what actions are in fact being taken? What concrete results are being obtained? Are the policies with which Britain is associating, and the related investments from Britain in fact contributing to the welfare of the Latin American people, as the Conservatives have claimed? Are our ambassadors helping to 'ensure democracy', as promised?

Conservatives after all are the first to demand returns for public expenditure, but doubtless their answers on these questions will continue to be evasive and misleading. Yet, their bluff should constantly be called and their contradictions fully exposed, at the same time as foundations are laid for progressive and socialist policies towards Latin America in the future.

THE EUROPEAN LABOUR MOVEMENT'S LATIN AMERICAN DILEMMA
DON THOMSON

The intensity of labour struggles in Latin America is now provoking heated debate within European labour international bureaucracies. What is at issue is the purpose of present day trade union internationalism and, above all, the idea of union 'economism' and its separation from political struggle.

Labour economism solidified with the growth of prosperity in post-war Europe with many unions shedding previous class-based political ideologies since, with the re-establishment of democracy, they could instead look to one political party or another to represent their social goals.

Substantial problems arise, however, when efforts are made to export this same union economism through the various international labour organisations into regions where there is massive poverty and no democratic process.

Latin America, more than elsewhere, illustrates this dilemma. There, worker struggles for basic social change have long transcended calls for better wages and shorter working hours. There is now abundant evidence that the attempted import of union economism is being deliberately used as a tool to contain or neutralise these struggles.

European labour leaders are now prepared to acknowledge that the repercussions of this have been an embarrassment for the international trade union movement, and in the past year efforts have been made to ameliorate this situation. While it is too early to predict the outcome, it is clear that what could be developing is the genesis of a new kind of worker internationalism radically different from that which exists at present. However, if it is to be sustained and developed, this movement will also certainly mean increased rank and file involvement. To date there has been none, and nor has it been encouraged by the labour bureaucracies.

US Unionism and Latin America

The origins of the present crisis reside to a great degree in the nature and style of US unionism and what is known as the US business-labour tradition. No account of European labour's dilemma is possible without an assessment of this phenomenon and its extension into Latin America.

The US labour movement has retained the old craft union mentality to a greater degree than any of its European counterparts. In the past this meant that labour leaders and bosses saw mutual advantage in combining forces to resist the organisation of the unskilled, blacks and women. From this developed the philosophy – expounded above all by Samuel Gompers, founder of the American Federation of Labour (AFL) – that labour had permanent advantage in identifying with the interests of the bosses. In essence, what was being propounded was the view that labour prospered when business prospered.

The logic of the business-labour tradition implied that just as labour would work to protect and defend US business interests at home they would do so overseas. Latin America was the first region to feel the effects of this.

During the Second World War the United States replaced Europe as Latin America's chief trading partner. US strategy revolved around securing raw materials necessary for the war and, since European markets were in ruins, making the subcontinent a dumping ground for surplus production. The government started a programme for this purpose organised under the Office of Inter-American Affairs (OIAA) headed by Nelson Rockefeller. It was through the OIAA that labour-capital cooperation in Latin America became institutionalised.

Rockefeller took up office in 1940 and one of his first acts was to form a labour advisory board. Later he revealed to a US Senate foreign relations committee that its prime purpose was to combat the Latin American Workers Confederation (CTAL) led by Vincent Lombardo Toledano, a pro-Communist Mexican trade unionist. The CTAL (which was dissolved in 1953) was threatening expropriation of foreign interests. Nonetheless, at that time it was recognised by the US State Department as the legitimate spokesman for Latin American labour.

The AFL, however, did not recognise the CTAL, and their own right-wing union contacts – particularly in Chile – formed an important part of Rockefeller's strategy: the creation of an opposing labour federation more amenable to US business interests.

In 1943, the AFL appointed Jay Lovestone to head its international department. He had been recruited by AFL president George Meany and both were fervent anti-Communists. Lovestone had previously been general secretary of the US Communist Party but, in a remarkable about-turn, he left the CP and developed an obsessional hatred for the Party. One of his first tasks was to create a Free Trade Union Committee (FTUC) expressly designed to combat overseas Communist unions. Although the FTUC was nominally under the control of the AFL, there was little participation by the executive and none at all by the membership. From the beginning there was direct contact with the State Department and later direct subservience to Cord Meyer's international division of the CIA.

In 1946, Lovestone secured the appointment of Serafino Romualdi to the FTUC. Romualdi, a former member of the Office of Strategic Services (OSS) – precursor to the CIA – began laying the groundwork for a new trade union federation in Latin America. In 1948, as a result of Romauldi's work, 156 trade unionists representing unions in 17 Latin American countries met in Lima formally to inaugurate the Inter-American Confederation of Labour (CIT).

Three years later the CIT gave way to the Inter-American Regional Organisation of Workers (ORIT), founded in Mexico City and including the major North American labour confederations. It was here that the present European labour connection was established. Shortly afterwards ORIT was to become the official western hemispheric wing of the International Confederation of Free Trade Unions (ICFTU), established in London in 1949.

The European unions, most of which were still in disarray as a result of the war, had little or no means at that stage of questioning the purpose of ORIT, still less of exercising effective control over it. For a crucial feature of this new federation was its pan-American nature which meant that the AFL was able to maintain control over the organisation and convert it into little less than a tool for the CIA.

The Beginnings of European Involvement

The European labour connection with ORIT began in earnest in 1951 when the AFL agreed to join the ICFTU which had set up its headquarters in Brussels. Formed as a breakaway social democratic group from the Communist controlled World Federation of Trade Unions (WFTU), its two main forces for many years were to be the AFL and the British TUC. And, in the scramble to win Third World affiliates into the ICFTU and away from the Communist sphere of influence, ORIT was quickly accepted into membership with few questions asked.

Within a few years, however, it became clear to the European affiliates that ORIT was, to a greater or lesser extent, bound up in US espionage efforts.

One example of this was the role ORIT played in helping to bring down the democratically elected government of Jacobo Arbenz in Guatemala in 1954. Arbenz had introduced a programme of land reform which threatened the US United Fruit Company, which included among its shareholders members of the AFL executive. Romualdi moved in and attempted to form a union to compete with and oppose the main workers' federation. He was ejected from the country following accusations that he was working for the CIA. The AFL, however, was already involved in a broader offensive: members of the unsuccessful dual union were linked up with a CIA-directed invasion force which overthrew the Arbenz government. Following the coup and the establishment of a military regime Romualdi moved back to reorganise the Guatemalan unions.

The European affiliates response to this was to demand a hearing on the funding and programmes of the ICFTU regional organisations. Ironically, this was welcomed by Lovestone and Meany who wanted such an enquiry so that they could complain about British and French reluctance to free their own colonies and permit the US unions to establish contacts with their colonial union bodies. The AFL team believed (correctly) that the TUC's overseas work was controlled by the Foreign Office and that, particularly in Africa, the TUC ethos of non-political unionism was being used as a pretext to crack down on unions led by members of independence movements. Lovestone and Meany argued that British unwillingness to decolonise was producing a climate in which the Communists would benefit by becoming identified with the anti-colonial struggle.

Matters came to head at the 1955 ICFTU congress in Vienna where Meany attacked colonialism and Soviet imperialism as being essentially similar. It was proposed there be a world-wide boycott of all goods produced by slave labour, i.e. all goods produced in nations under Soviet or colonial domination. This was bitterly opposed by the British, French, Belgian and Dutch unionists. Although the proposal was defeated, the US had successfully directed criticism and enquiry away from their Latin American operations.

The main controversy that was to develop in the subsequent period was over ICFTU policy in Africa and was fought out by the US and British. The latter had little political or commercial interest in Latin America and were inclined, therefore, to concentrate on defending their African role against the growing US offensive there.

The TUC and other European affiliates hoped that with the merger in 1955 of the AFL and the traditionally more militant Congress of Industrial Relations (CIO), which was closer in attitude to the European labour movement, that the latter would be able to make an impression upon the foreign policies of the AFL leadership. In reality, however, the CIO failed to exert any influence upon the AFL-CIO international department.

The European affiliates began to pick up more disturbing rumours about ORIT through the CIO and Canadian Labour Congress, but again firm action was hindered by the continuing battle between the US and the TUC over policy in Africa. Meany responded to ICFTU suspicions about ORIT by offering to place a Briton in the ORIT hierarchy, providing that Irving Brown — a CIA agent — was given responsibility for ICFTU activities in Africa. The deal was turned down. Once again the US had successfully suppressed European labour action over ORIT — but worries increased when in 1957 the ICFTU created a Solidarity Fund that began financing ORIT activities.

The Growing European Dilemma

By now, the US labour machine for Latin America had developed into an impressive organisation. It pivoted around the axis of the AFL-CIO international department, the CIA, labour attaches (none of whom could be appointed without Lovestone's consent), aided by various academic institutions which assisted in the collection of data on labour movements. Assisted by ICFTU funding, an ORIT training school was established in Mexico and students were closely monitored by the local CIA station for possible recruitment.

The structure of ORIT reflected its origins. Many of its affiliates were government-controlled or approved union centres, often with a very small real membership. Their existence, however, served as a pretext for governments to close down competing and more representative unions while still preserving a democratic facade.

By the early 1960s ORIT began employing a number of right-wing Cuban exiles. This policy followed one of Romualdi's sorties — an attempt to make an arrangement that would allow the Cuban Workers' Federation (CTC) the right to exist freely in exchange for them neutralising attempts by organised labour to overthrow the Batista regime. When Castro came to power Romualdi attempted to meet the new regime but was instead thrown out of Cuba. This setback provoked the AFL-CIO to speed up its Latin America labour programme and reveal the true purpose of its work — the protection of US corporate interests.

In 1961 — to the shock of the ICFTU European affiliates — the AFL-CIO began accepting funds from government and big business in order to start an independent labour programme for Latin America — the American Institute for Free Labour Development (AIFLD). J.P. Grace of W.R. Grace and Co., a multinational with huge holdings in Latin America, was appointed chairman (a position he still holds) while numerous other big companies began financing AIFLD activities.

Romualdi moved from ORIT to AIFLD, which began working together on a widespread programme of disruption and subversion among Latin American labour. In 1964, for instance, an ORIT employee, Andrew McClellan (who now heads the AFL-CIO Latin America programme), was instrumental, through the labour unions, in organising the coup which brought down the democratic government of Juan Bosch in the Dominican Republic.

In Brazil, both ORIT and AIFLD gave training to unionists in key industrial sectors — such as communications workers — thus paving the way for the military coup in 1964 and the subsequent crushing of the labour movement. AIFLD director William Doherty later boasted: 'What happened in Brazil did not just happen, it was planned and months in advance. Many of the trade union leaders, some of whom were trained in our own institutes, were involved.'

By now the ICFTU European affiliates were in a serious dilemma. The Solidarity Fund had been captured by the US and was chaired by George Meany despite opposition from the TUC. Money was still being directed to ORIT and it seemed as if any effective action against it would entail the departure of the AFL-CIO from the ICFTU. Few were willing to force the issue to the point where the ICFTU would be broken up in this manner.

There were additional problems. The other major force inside the ICFTU was the TUC which was compromised by connections with its own government. The TUC, for instance, was believed to be implicated, along with the AFL-CIO, in the coup that brought down Cheddi Jagan in British Guyana in 1961. The TUC was also concerned that if it forced the Latin America issue too hard it would not merely drive the AFL-CIO out of the ICFTU but also encourage them to build up their own independent and competing labour programmes in areas of British interest.

What the ICFTU did attempt was to hold on to the idea (preposterous though it turned out to be) that ORIT in some way remained independent from the by now much more powerful AIFLD programme.

In 1968, a US Senate inquiry identified ORIT with the downfall of governments in Guatemala, Guyana, the Dominican Republic and Brazil. Despite this, the ICFTU (its Nordic affiliates excepted) continued funding the ORIT. However, the same year, following more fierce battles about control of the ICFTU Solidarity Fund, the AFL-CIO stormed out of the ICFTU and greatly expanded their own independent programmes in the Third World.

The problem of ORIT was now given a new twist. The ICFTU was desperately anxious to win back the AFL-CIO, but firm action over ORIT would reduce the chance of this − a problem the Americans were able to exploit to the full. There were to be important consequences for the ICFTU.

In 1973, ORIT and the AIFLD, working together in a programme of political destabilization, were instrumental in supporting the coup which brought down the constitutional Allende government in Chile. The truck owners and maritime workers, both secretly financed through these US-controlled labour structures, played a key role in this operation.

It is significant that neither the TUC nor other ICFTU European affiliates have ever denied this charge. What is also true, however, is that the Latin American connection had by then become something of a nightmare for European labour bosses. Whatever excuses might be put forward for their association with ORIT – and there are some – it also has to be said that it is inconceivable that the connection would have remained for long had the rank and file had the slightest idea about what was going on.

Towards a New Trade Union Internationalism?

In 1975, following the ICFTU congress in Mexico City – and largely through the initiative of Jack Jones, TUC international chairman – the ICFTU ordered the closure of the ORIT training college, regained control of the building and handed it over to the CTM, the major Mexican labour federation. At the same time, the ICFTU unsuccessfully attempted to convert ORIT into an exclusively Latin American organisation. The AFL-CIO, however, exerted financial and other pressure on ORIT to destroy this possibility.

In the same year, the ICFTU finally decided to cease funding ORIT, although it still remains the official regional affiliate which effectively deprives the European labour movement of contact with the authentic Latin American labour movement.

Since then the ICFTU has suspended three of the government-controlled ORIT affiliates – in Paraguay, El Salvador and Guatemala. This action, taken at the 1979 ICFTU world congress, is the first of its kind in the organisation's 30 year history and it is now considering suspending the Uruguay affiliate. An equally significant episode – one which captures the essence of the dilemma of European labour over Latin America – occurred in the Autumn of 1979 when ICFTU general secretary Otto Kerston met with ORIT leaders in Caracas.

He told them that they were an 'embarrassment' to the free trade union movement and then argued that in the absence of democratic processes it was right for unions to engage in political struggle to protect their members. He then added: 'It's about time some national trade union centres in the West who enjoy the luxury of democratic processes recognise this reality.'

Kerston's last remark was almost certainly directed at the TUC. For years the TUC was the only significant potential countervailing force to the AFL-CIO in the ICFTU (although today the German DGB is an important force). It is clear, however, that the

TUC was itself compromised by government connections and greatly pre-occupied with its own territorial sphere of interest. There is more than a hint that the TUC hoped that passivity on the Latin America question might wean the AFL-CIO away from interference in British areas of interest.

The problem goes deeper, however, for even if there had been no AFL-CIO activity in Latin America it is clear that the TUC and some of the other European unions centres, who hold fast to the idea of non-political unionism, would still have been faced with numerous problems in the subcontinent.

Ideology has played a dominant role in the history of Latin American trade unionism and numerous unions are organised as political forces. With one third of the population in the wage-earning sector, combined with the phenomenon of radical peasant league organisations seeking recovery of their land from the land-lord class, the union movement in Latin America is very much larger and more potent than its counterparts in other Third World continents. Many unions have adopted programmes for the ex-propriation of industry and land and, with many Latin American countries under right-wing military dictatorships, this has made them prime targets for repression while placing them at the fore-front of political struggle.

The single strongest Latin American regional federation is now the Confederation of Latin American Workers (CLAT) based in Caracas and founded in 1961. CLAT now has 35 national labour centres in Latin America and the Caribbean. It is also the strongest regional affiliate of the formerly Catholic and Brussels-based World Confederation of Labour (WCL), smallest of the three world internationals.

CLAT — and the WCL in turn — has adopted an avowedly class-based programme which includes expropriation of foreign capital and rejection of both Soviet and US 'imperialism'. US subversion of CLAT has taken two main forms: attempted pene-tration of the hierarchy (CLAT now largely recruits headquarters staff from unionists released from prison); and, more recently, the Inter-American Foundation, a US 'independent government agency', has been engaged in trying to woo some CLAT affiliates by a heavy programme of financing.

Because of the poverty of so many of its affiliates CLAT still depends on external funding, this coming mainly from the Konrad Adenauer Stiftung in West Germany which serves the

34

Christian Democrat movement. This remains a source of controversy and there are allegations that CLAT deliberately withholds this cash from affiliates unless they toe the headquarters line.

Radical opponents of CLAT complain about its 'centralism' and argue that aid is withheld from affiliates who embark on direct political action. CLAT responds that the experience of the past decade is that the Latin American revolutionary strategies have failed and that the need is to regroup and rebuild instead of engaging in political 'adventurism' which could put many lives at stake.

What is clear, however, is that in Latin America — as elsewhere in the Third World — the most divisive force among unions now centres around the question of foreign funding. At present there is a marked tendency for unions to move towards independence from the various world internationals and in Latin America recently there has been an abortive attempt by some national centres to create a new federation for the subcontinent.

In none of these or other developments, however, is there any comfort for the European labour bureaucracies. They are at one in wanting to oppose Communism but cannot agree on what they want to achieve in its place. The non-political ethos of the TUC has remained dominant and wholly inappropriate for the Latin American labour movement which has no alternative but to engage in political struggle.

Now, with repression widespread throughout the subcontinent, there are growing signs that the European labour bureaucracies are experiencing a crisis of conscience. At the 1979 ICFTU world congress in Madrid an emotional appeal was made to the WCL to amalgamate with the ICFTU. Some — particularly the Dutch — believe this would be a way of solving the ORIT problem and perhaps even of linking up with at least some of the CLAT affiliates. The WCL — prompted by CLAT — flatly rejected this overture. Nonetheless, the signs are that a battle is developing inside the ICFTU over the basic issue of union internationalism.

The indications are that the more radical elements inside the ICFTU are beginning to win this battle. A powerful plea for a socialist and democratic approach — the 'ideological heritage from which we draw our strength' — won widespread support at the 1979 ICFTU world congress. The ICFTU's traditional anti-Communist platform is anyway largely irrelevant in the Latin American subcontinent where the Communist-controlled WFTU has limited union support and, indeed, following the coup in Chile nowhere to establish headquarters for its Latin American regional wing.

Nonetheless, considerable problems still face the Western trade union movements in their relations with their Latin American counterparts. The Canadian Labour Congress (CLC), which nominally shares powers of decision on the ORIT executive, has acknowledged that ORIT is indeed a tool of the CIA. The CLC is now pressing the ICFTU to insist that the AFL-CIO leave ORIT or, alternatively, to abandon ORIT itself. They concede that ORIT has become so discredited that even if the US departed European unions would be unlikely to want to fund the organisation. As far as the CLC is concerned ORIT will have to survive by its own efforts or go under.

The irony, however, is that it is now more likely that the AFL-CIO will assume formal control of ORIT and simply put an end to the European connection. This course of action was recommended in a 1975 report on US Latin American labour activities commissioned by USAID, the main funding source for AFL-CIO overseas work. The report argued that ORIT had become little more than a conference centre because the more powerful AIFLD had taken over most organising work. It recommended that some of this work – and AIFLD cash – be transferred to ORIT. These cash transfers have already started, suggesting that the next stage of the plan – ending the European connection – could well happen.

TUC General Council members admit that they could face problems and be left without a single union affiliate in Latin America. Unlike the Swedes or Dutch, the TUC is making no effort to link with Latin American unions outside the ORIT-AIFLD axis. Their lack of options springs from their historic belief that trade union internationalism should be non-political. This was most clearly enunciated in 1945 by the TUC's Sir Walter Citrine when he said the only way diverse union national centres could work together internationally would be by sticking to an economic approach.

The world, however, has changed radically since then. Citrine's argument was employed mainly to check Communist influence over the WFTU which for four years managed to combine union centres in both Eastern and Western blocs. Today, particularly in the Third World, both the Western and Eastern trade union blocs are increasingly being lumped together as part of the phenomenon of imperialism. The crucial issue is not the East-West conflict but rather the way governments, whatever their political complexion, have sought to contain or control trade union internationalism. It is a measure of governments' success in this field that the TUC can justify staff transfers to the Foreign Office on the grounds that they have to learn about 'international diplomacy', or that the Communists have kept quiet about the ICFTU's Latin American connections because of 'detente'.

In spite of this, however, there are many fighting with courage and vision, even within the official structures, to create a new internationalism that is both socialist and democratic. For them, the struggles of the Latin American working class have been a major inspiration. Whether or not this can be translated into a commitment towards real union democracy so that trade unionists in the Northern hemisphere can obtain information -- and therefore control – over their respective international programmes remains to be seen.

EUROPEAN-LATIN AMERICAN RELATIONS: A LATIN AMERICAN VIEW
ALBERTO ORLANDI

Economic relations between Latin America and Western Europe have been considerably influenced by the world-wide intensification of international trade and financial links, a process commonly referred to as the increasing internationalization of the world economy. However, within both regions there have been profound changes over the last 25 years which, in turn, are changing the nature of such relations.

Latin America seeks from North-South relations patterns of external trade and finance which favour rather than hinder, as has often been the case in the past, the attainment of the basic goals of accelerating economic and social development and strengthening national independence.

The Latin America that is today striving, to a certain extent successfully, to secure a new international division of labour is not the same Latin America of the immediate post-war period. There have been significant social and economic structural transformations in the region's process of development since then. Among these are the increasing importance of the urban middle class, the overall improvement of manpower skill levels, the expansion of the internal rate of savings and the deepening of the industrialization process, which has extended to all sectors of industry and has led, in various countries, to the development of a sizeable manufacturing export capacity accompanied by increased competitiveness in world markets.

It is nonetheless true that, by and large, income disparities have widened, both between and within countries. In general, Latin America has been persistently affected by a lack of harmony between economic growth on the one hand and social development on the other. Large sectors of the population, both urban and rural, still suffer from extreme poverty, while Latin American economies still cannot provide adequate employment for all their citizens. Last but not least, development goals are hindered in many countries by the persistence of severe external difficulties.

Latin America, in other words, still belongs to the developing world, and needs vigorous co-operation in order to solve its acute internal problems.

Trade

In this field it is worth recalling that Latin American industrialization strategies based on a high degree of protection of internal markets, which had been predominant in most countries in the 1950s, were substantially modified around the mid 1960s. Various countries in the region gradually reduced their tariff barriers, while at the same time implementing comprehensive programmes of export promotion.

Nevertheless, in 1976 the proportion of manufactures in total Latin American exports to all destinations was still only 14%, the remaining 86% being accounted for by primary commodities.[1]

The weight of non-oil primary commodities in total exports, and their sharp fall as a percentage of world trade, help explain the drastic decrease of non-OPEC Latin American participation in world trade between 1950 and 1977 in terms of exports (from 10.4% to 4.5%) and imports (from 9.0% to 4.8%). Even more astonishing, however, is that Latin America, as well as all other developing regions, even lost ground to the developed countries in the export of primary commodities themselves: between 1955 and 1977, this was the case for each of the four groups of primary commodities: food and beverages, agricultural raw materials, minerals and non-ferrous metals.

Latin America's share in the total imports of Western Europe decreased from 7.3% to 3.2% between 1955 and 1977, while there was a similar trend in Western Europe's exports to Latin America (down from 7.0% to 3.4%). This decline, which incidentally was not quite as sharp as that of other developing regions (except OPEC), was essentially brought about by an unprecedented increase in Western European intra-regional trade, which, over the same period, rose from 54.8% to 65.4% of the total. In the case of the EEC, intra-regional trade represented more than half of the Community's total trade in 1977.

Latin America's interest in a more dynamic evolution of its trade with Europe lies in the importance of Europe as a trading partner for the region, which is obviously much greater than the reverse[2], and in the importance of the external sector in general for the achievement of its overall development goals.

The structure of trade between the two regions is very un-balanced: Latin America's exports to Europe are mostly primary products (76.7%) while Europe's exports to Latin America are overwhelmingly manufactured goods (90.4%).[3] This phenomenon, which should in no way be regarded as God-given and unchangeable, is partly influenced by the different resource endownments of the two regions. However, other elements are also important in explaining the persistence of such imbalance, such as the prevailing inertia in international trade, and the emergence of protectionist trends, mainly on the part of the EEC, which adversely affect Latin America's export potential in items which are of considerable importance to several countries in the region.[4]

The EEC countries are faced, in different degrees, with balance of payments problems, unemployment and inflation. It is not a question of disregarding the seriousness of these difficulties, but rather of pointing out that:

— the benefit of protectionist policies for the EEC countries is certainly less, comparatively speaking, than the harm they do to Latin America;

— by barring imports of manufactures, the EEC reduced the purchasing power of exporting countries, which, in turn, decreases their level of imports (boomerang effect);

— by unduly protecting industries which are uncompetitive in international markets, the EEC postpones its own industrial restructuring, thereby inducing harmful consequences in terms of less dynamic industrial development and inflationary pressures.

Furthermore, it is worth recalling that in the not too distant past Latin America was induced, on the grounds of free trade principles, to accept trade flows that benefitted the industrialized countries, but did not necessarily contribute to the region's own economic and social development. The consumption, accumulation and production patterns generated by these flows did not coincide with the needs of Latin American countries.

It is ironic to note that, as free trade turns to their disadvantage, the developed countries do not hesitate to break away from those principles which they were so quick to advocate in the past.

For the reasons outlined, Western Europe, and the EEC in particular, should not try to protect its market against those Latin American manufactured products which have proved to be competitive in world trade. Giving a substantial boost to these exports will not only have a favourable effect on social and economic development in the region but will also, by easing Latin America's balance of payments problem, enhance the region's purchasing power to the advantage of European exporters of goods with a high technology content, which cannot be substituted by domestic production.

Finally, the particular problem of Latin America's exclusion from preferential trade zones granted by the EEC in Africa, the Pacific and the Mediterranean should be noted.[5] While not ignoring the EEC's interest in granting trade advantages to the least developed countries, especially where colonial links existed in the past, such preferences should not adversely affect the trading position of other developing countries, especially as not all the countries which benefit from the EEC's special preferences have a lower level of development than many Latin American countries.

Direct Private Investment (DPI)

This is another very important aspect of economic relations between Latin America and Europe. Latin America represented 15% of total Western European accumulated DPI to all destinations in 1976, ranking first among the developing regions. For the whole of Latin America, the share of European accumulated DPI increased between 1967 and 1976 from 23% to 26% of the total, while over the same period the USA saw its share decline from 66% to 61%. In other words, the gap between the two is gradually being reduced. In Brazil, Europe already represents a higher share of total accumulated DPI than the USA.[6]

European DPI is mostly directed towards the industrial sector, producing for a protected internal market. From the European point of view, this constitutes a process of 'export substitution', which is of considerable importance as, according to recent estimates, the value of production of European enterprises in Latin America is much higher than that of European exports of manufactures to the region.

Another indication of the importance of investment in the economic relations between the two regions is given by comparing the figures for trade (only 3.4% of total European imports came from Latin America in 1977) with those for European DPI in the region (15% of the total in 1976).

Latin America is attractive to foreign investors for a number of reasons, among which can be singled out the size of the market, relatively low labour costs, and the availability of natural resources, including energy. However, strong doubts have been expressed about the contribution of foreign investment to the attainment of national development goals.

In the specific case of Latin America, the ultimate net balance of payments effect of foreign investment is heavily on the negative side, owing to the increase in imports which these generate as well as annual payments for interest, remittances of profits, royalties and technical assistance.

Transnational enterprises have also been criticised for their behaviour in other fields, including restrictive practices with regard to exports, intra-firm pricing policies, their negative effect on the capacity for creating indigenous technology, control over natural resources, etc.

As a result of the widespread concern about the net effect of DPI on national economies, some countries have reacted by setting up legislative bodies regulating the conditions under which foreign investment can be established (e.g. Mexico and the Andean Pact countries), while other countries have preferred to negotiate with transnational enterprises on a case-by-case basis (Brazil). Finally, a handful of countries have reverted to fully-fledged laissez-faire, welcoming foreign investment more or less unconditionally (Chile and, to a lesser extent, Argentina).

There can be no doubt that, when guided by legislation and/or case-by-case negotiation, DPI can make an important and sometimes vital contribution to the attainment of industrial goals in specific fields. This contribution is potentially most valuable in the fields of technology, access to markets for manufactured goods, and organizational matters.

European enterprises have in certain cases proved to be more flexible than their US counterparts, probably owing to their minority status in the region. We believe that their eagerness to increase their participation in Latin America should be paralleled by a clear willingness to improve the quality of their partnership with Latin American countries or enterprises along the following lines:

— disaggregation of the technology package should be allowed so the recipient country can purchase only that portion of it which is not available locally;

— the export of goods produced in co-operation with foreign capital should not be hindered; on the contrary, the foreign enterprise should make its international marketing network available for this purpose;

— excess profits should be eliminated through more suitable behaviour of foreign enterprises as regards transfer pricing, technical assistance, royalties, etc.;

— foreign enterprises should abstain from interfering in the social and political institutions of recipient countries;

— the net financial contribution of foreign enterprises should be significantly higher.

Financing

With respect to external financing, the situation of Latin America has undergone important changes in the last decade or so. The balance of payments current account deficit rose very quickly, and official sources of financing gradually lost ground, being replaced by private flows. Accordingly, terms and conditions of payment deteriorated and the external debt increased dramatically.

Europe's share in total external financing of the region decreased between 1970 and 1974 from 32% to 25%, in spite of a notable increase in absolute figures.

With respect to official development assistance (ODA), Latin America received only 5.6% of the European total between 1969 and 1975, and more than half of this figure originated from the Federal Republic of Germany. Possible lines of action to improve the current situation could be based on the following points:

— the improvement of Latin America's access to medium and long-term private capital markets;

— the attainment, on the part of the developed countries, of the internationally recognized goals for ODA, and its more equitable distribution among developing areas, reversing the trend towards the exclusion of Latin America from these flows;

— the improvement and enlargement of existing compensatory financing services.

Future Relations

This represents a brief attempt to analyse the state of economic relations between Europe and Latin America in the fields of trade, investment and financing and the problems and possibilities of co-operation on these matters.

These points deserve more detailed treatment, and moreover, although they have been dealt with separately for analytical purposes, they are closely inter-related.

The problems affecting economic relations between Europe and Latin America should therefore be discussed, and solutions found, at a global level. In this connection, the great interest shown by European countries in Latin American internal markets − both for exports and investment − is in clear contradiction with their failure to take into consideration the internal and external needs of the Latin American economies.

Footnotes

1. This figure would be 47% if fuels were excluded and 75% if the total trade of Latin American OPEC countries (Venezuela and Ecuador) were excluded.
2. 25.2% of total Latin American exports went to W. Europe in 1977 (down from 30.5% in 1955).
3. This percentage would be higher still if an estimate of the trade in arms were included.
4. These include meat, leather and footwear, textiles, steel products, electronic items, vehicles, etc.
5. Not without singling out the notable exception of those Caribbean countries which are members of the Lomé agreement.
6. The conduct of European direct investors in Brazil is examined in an article on page 45 of this review.

EUROPEAN DIRECT INVESTMENT AND THE BRAZILIAN ECONOMIC MODEL
PETER-UWE SCHLIEMANN

1979 was a turbulent year in Brazil. Inflation reached almost 80%, the foreign debt became the world's largest (about US$50 billion) and strikes spread throughout the country. A partial political amnesty allowed exiles such as former governor Miguel Arraes and other leading opposition politicans to return to Brazil. Their return, however, contrasts sharply with that of Professor Delfim Neto to his former position as Brazil's planning minister and 'overlord'.

For Miguel Arraes, Brazil is 'an occupied nation'. 'The dominant classes . . . are allied with the external exploiters and conserve the behaviour and mentality of primitive occupiers', he argues. For Delfim Neto, on the other hand, foreign direct investments are welcome in order to bring about increased output; the priority is to increase the size of the 'cake' and then worry about its distribution.

It is therefore pertinent to analyse the conduct and influence of foreign direct investors in Brazil and to discuss how they relate to the country's current problems.

Overall, foreign direct investments (FDIs) account for less than 5% of the country's total capital stock, the balance belonging to locally owned enterprises, including about 520 state enterprises. This is often stressed by government officials in an attempt to play down the magnitude of FDIs in Brazil and the consequent denationalization of its economy. It is, however, not the amount of ownership which determines the influence of foreign direct investors in Brazil, but the question of control. This enables one to understand further Miguel Arraes' point about domination. In short, it is the denationalization of the Brazilian economy which is at stake and its broader implications of a net outflow of foreign exchange, and the loss of the country's autonomy in deciding how, when, where and to whose benefit the country's resources should be allocated.

The Investment Climate

The inflow of FDIs over time is an interesting thermometer of the investment climate in Brazil. Table 1, indicating the inflow of FDIs from 1947 to 1978, shows that foreign direct investors have reacted rationally to changes in the Brazilian economic and political environment.

The concept of 'associated development' — i.e. strong reliance on FDIs — was first applied by the transitional government of Cafe Filho (1954-56). Eugenio Gudin as finance minister, and Octavio Gouveia de Bulhoes as head of SUMOC (the predecessor of the Central Bank), introduced extremely attractive incentives for FDIs and created prospects for growth.

The Kubitschek government which followed (1956-61) continued the formula of 'associated development'. Furthermore, it emphasized the slogan of achieving 50 years of industrialization in only 5 years, implemented economic development plans and created such executive institutions as GEIA (the Executive Group for the Automobile Industry). In short, the government offered foreign direct investors full support and, most important, suitable conditions for growth. The reaction of these investors to such a 'friendly atmosphere' is fully reflected in the increased inflow during this period.

On the other hand, in the later Goulart government (1962-64), in which the balance of power was less markedly in favour of the Brazilian 'internationalists', the inflow fell to US$58 million in 1963-64. This clearly reflects the more restrictive measures that the Goulart government introduced toward foreign direct investors. On the one hand, Brazilian capital remittance laws were tightened and reinvested profits were treated as national capital. On the other hand, Leonel Brizola, the governor of the state of Rio Grande do Sul, unilaterally nationalized the state's public utility subsidiaries of ITT and AMFORP. In due course, foreign direct investors called for the implementation of the Hickenlooper Amendment (which allows the US government to take economic sanctions against countries which threaten US business interests) and President Kennedy's personal intervention.

After the right-wing military coup of 1964 the inflow of FDIs increased again, despite the tough recession policies of the Castello Branco government, with Roberto Campos as planning minister and Octavio Bulhoes as finance minister. FDI inflow,

Table 1 — Inflow of Foreign Direct Investments in Brazil — 1947-78

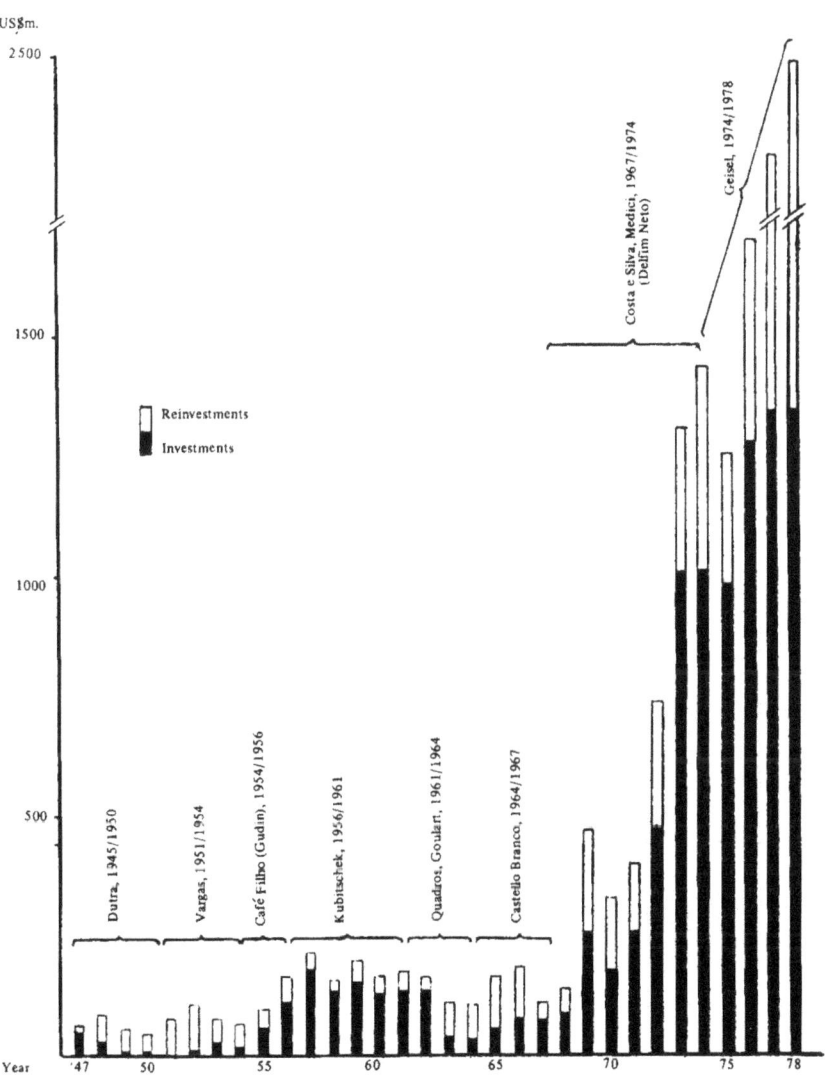

Source: *Boletim do Banco Central do Brasil*

47

however, achieved its relatively highest increases over the period 1968-74, when Delfim Neto was finance minister and promoted growth rates averaging 10% a year.

So far the inflow of the FDIs has been analysed overall. The next sections will identify those sectors in which foreign direct investments are most strongly represented and will highlight some major differences between foreign direct investors by country of origin (mainly British and German direct investors).

The Pattern of Investment

In 1974 only 4% of total British direct investments overseas (except oil, insurance and banking) were located in South and Central America, as against 35% in 1930. In the 19th century Britain had been by far the most important direct investor in the region but in the 20th century, with the expansion of other capitalist countries such as Germany and the USA, Britain gradually lost that predominance.

Whereas in 1950 the British still held 3rd place after the USA and Canada among Brazil's foreign direct investors, by 1978 she had dropped to sixth place. By then West Germany accounted for 14% and took second place behind the USA (30%). Japanese and Swiss direct investors competed for third place, each holding 11%.

Between 1939 and 1977, as British direct investments in Brazil sharply decreased, industry gradually increased its share in the country's GNP from 19% to 37% while agriculture's share decreased from 26% to 11%. Moreover, within industry, the dynamic sectors such as chemicals and pharmaceuticals, transport equipment, metallurgy, machinery and electrical equipment, increased their share from 26% to 50% over the period 1950 to 1968.

Table 2 shows that it is precisely these more dynamic sectors which account for 56% of all foreign direct investments. A further 21% is directed toward other manufacturing sectors such as textiles and tobacco.

Only 56% of British direct investments are to be found in the manufacturing sectors with only 35% in the more dynamic ones, as against 90% and 82%, respectively, for German direct investments. Moreover, the British are almost completely absent from the Brazilian automobile industry, which has enjoyed the most spectacular growth rates over the past 25 years. It is only in the

Table 2 — Foreign Direct Investments by Sectors and Countries (as at 30.6.78)
(percentages)

Sectors	Total	West Germany	United Kingdom	USA	Japan
Chemicals and Pharmaceuticals	17	10	24	23	3
Vehicles and Parts	13	35	1	12	4
Metallurgy and Steel Works	9	15	4	4	16
Mechanics	9	14	4	11	10
Electrical and Communication Equipment	8	8	2	10	11
Total 'Dynamic' Industries	56	82	35	60	44
All other Processing Industries	21	8	21*	22	30**
Total Manufacturing	77	90	56	82	74
Services	17	7	41	12	20
Agriculture, Minerals and Others	6	3	3	6	6
Total	100	100	100	100	100
— of which: investments	66	70	70	62	93
reinvestments	34	30	38	40	7
Total in US$ million	12,200	1,700	610	3,700	1,200

Source: Boletim do Banco Central do Brasil
* Includes 11% Tobacco
** Includes 11% Textiles.

chemical and pharmaceutical sectors that the British have a significant presence in the more dynamic sectors. US direct investments in Brazil declined from 44% in 1950 to 30% in 1978, but despite this, American predominance is still remarkable, especially in the chemical sector.

Major differences between foreign direct investors do exist, but the general pattern indicates that the majority of FDIs lie in industry and, within industry, in the so-called 'modern' sectors, which until the present have grown most rapidly.

Another aspect worth noting is the association of FDIs with industries dominated by a few companies. In their report to a US Senate sub-committee in 1977, Connor and Mueller confirmed that in the cases of Mexico and Brazil market concentration has a direct influence on a firm's profits, as has 'the relative dominance of individual firms' and the 'height of entry barriers'.[1] Out of the 172 American subsidiaries which they studied in Brazil two-thirds were located in industries in which the four leading firms held a market share of 69%. In the automibile industry, for example, a few foreign companies controlled over 90% of the total annual output of about 1 million cars. In 1978 Volkswagen held an individual share of 45% of the passenger car market while Mercedes-Benz held a market share of 51% for trucks over 3 tons and 96% for buses.

In order to reach such oligopolistic market positions foreign direct investors have often in the past divided up the market between them. For example, 'in 1953 Fiat and VW came to an understanding that Fiat would stay out of Brazil if VW would reciprocate by doing the same as far as Argentina was concerned', according to the *Financial Times* (15.1.1980). This arrangement broke down only after 21 years, when 'Fiat penetrated Brazil with a version of the 127 car which quickly captured 10% of that market'.

Furthermore, in a laissez-faire environment such as prevails in Brazil it is little wonder that foreign direct investors also mainly entered the market by taking over locally owned enterprises. This strategy and some of its consequences are illustrated by the case of British American Tobacco (BAT).

British American Tobacco in Brazil

BAT is Brazil's largest British direct investor, holding approximately a quarter of all British direct investments in Brazil. In Brazil, as in many other countries, BAT has used the strategy of take-overs in all three sectors in which it is integrated — the manufacture of cigarettes, cigarette tissues and cigarette machinery.

BAT took over Souza Cruz Comercio e Industria in 1914 and Cigarros Castelloes, which was until then Brazil's largest cigarette manufacturer, in 1955. In the manufacturing of cigarette tissues BAT took over the Compania Industrial de Papel Pirahy in 1936 with the aim of developing it into a cigarette tissue mill. Through this move BAT was gradually able to gain control over its competitors in the cigarette manufacturing industries, given their dependence on the manufacture of cigarette tissues. Finally, Molins Limited, in which BAT held a 25% share, started production of machinery for the tobacco industry in Brazil in 1961, a year after it had acquired a 50% share in Baker Perkins do Brasil.

With the sole exception of the latter case — which was a British owned company — the outcome has been a direct increase in the denationalization of the respective sectors. In acting in this way BAT has carefully avoided the additional output which the construction of new plants would have required in an industry which was already well-established as a locally owned one. Only after it had captured the lion's share of the market and become a price leader, did BAT engage in the construction of a new plant in Uberlandia. This plant, which opened in late 1978, will eventually be capable of producing 3 billion cigarettes a month. The size and modernity of this plant, the distribution network which the company has built up directly serving over 350,000 sales outlets, and the powerful control the company exerts over the supply of raw tobacco, can together be expected to constitute an effective barrier to competition.

It is not surprising that only multinationals have been able to contend with such barriers. By the end of the 1970s BAT held a market share of 84% and most of the remaining 16% was held by two US companies, R.J. Reynolds Tabacco do Brasil Ltd and Philip Morris Brasileira de Cigarros. The fact that BAT shares the market with these enterprises, which only entered in the 1970s, should reduce the risk of future governments in Brazil nationalizing the cigarette industry. In other words, if a more nationalistic government in Brazil wanted to nationalize this highly concentrated industry it would have to contend not only with the UK as a foreign direct investor's home country but also with the USA, which would certainly make things more complicated for the Brazilians.

This use of take-overs as a strategy of entry is not confined to BAT. Schliemann found that 50% of a sample of 18 British enterprises used this method of entry.[2]

The leading foreign direct investors have benefitted handsomely from behaving in the manner described above. BAT, for example, transferred over US$80 million out of Brazil in the form of profits and dividends during a period of only 10½ years (January 1965-July 1975) as against under US$3 million which it had brought into Brazil since the date of its registration in the country.[3] Moreover, in Brazilian congressional hearings in 1970, 1976 and 1978 on the activities of multinational companies operating in the country the ability of foreign direct investors to circumvent Brazilian income tax has also been demonstrated: for instance, through the use of payments for technology (as in the case of Volkswagen do Brasil), inter-affiliate interest payments and transfer-pricing.

Foreign direct investors in Brazil have also extended their influence and power through the cultivation of close contacts amongst Brazilian political figures.

Foreign Companies and Political Influence in Brazil

Newfarmer has carried out a study of these political linkages, looking at the inter-relationship between military or political figures and company directors as indicators of potential political influence. He points out that from his research within the electrical industry the clearest examples of what he calls 'political interlocks' are in the telecommunications companies. 'Siemens, Nippon Electrical Company, Standard Electric (ITT), and Ericson have directors who hold or have held government posts'.[4] The difficulty, of course, lies in proving exactly how such political linkages operate, as without precise and inside knowledge firm inferences are risky. Newfarmer was aware of this in his work on the electrical sector, and the same problem applies to the example below, that of BAT's subsidiary, Souza Cruz.

On 1 January 1965, when Octavio Gouveia de Bulhoes was

finance minister Law No.4502 came into force which allowed companies, including the tobacco industry, to cease paying sales tax in advance. Souza Cruz, already then a leader in the cigarette industry and one of the country's largest sales tax payers, could now pay its sales tax after invoicing with an average of 22½ days grace. While the company continued to sell its cigarettes for cash, this effectively meant that the Brazilian government gave Souza Cruz an interest-free 'loan' of an estimated US$100 million 'repayable' only in the very unlikely case of a new law annulling the former one, a fact which was pointed in the Brazilian congressional hearings on multinationals in 1976[5].

In 1968, Octavio Gouveia de Bulhoes and Mario Henrique Simonsen, respectively the former and future finance ministers, joined the supervisory board of Souza Cruz. Although Simonsen emphasized that both he and Bulhoes joined only after the introduction of this law which so greatly benefitted Souza Cruz in particular, certain doubts remain. In Newfarmer's words: 'why do companies leave themselves open to public suspicion if no influence comes from these relationships?'. In the case of Souza Cruz, moreover, this question has remained unanswered since further investigations were discontinued when the main investigator – federal deputy Lysaneas Maciel – lost his political position by presidential decree in April 1976, shortly after having raised the issue in Congress.

Other kinds of linkage include the tendency of foreign direct investors to grant economic benefits to politically influential Brazilians. One example, which was cited in the congressional hearings of 1970, was the case of VW which nominated several such people to be its concessionaires throughout Brazil.[6]

A foreign company which is well known for dealing with the government in Brazil 'on the basis of influence', as one researcher has put it, is the Canadian firm, BRASCAN. Its interest in Brazil dates back to 1889 when it founded, in association with Brazilian capital, the Sao Paulo Railway Light & Power Co. BRASCAN's linkages, both international and national, are remarkable. For example, Hennan Abs, honorary president of the Deutsche Bank, sits on its European advisory committee, while Antonio Galotti, one of its vice-presidents and senior corporate officers, is an influential Brazilian lawyer. However, the real basis of BRASCAN's widespread influence in Brazil seems to lie in the simple fact that it was, for so many decades, a training house for many of today's influential managers, engineers, lawyers, ministers and others.

For BRASCAN this far-reaching integration within the international and national business community has paid handsome dividends. The most striking example can be found in the conditions of the recent nationalization of Light Servicos de Eletricidade SA, which was its largest subsidiary in Brazil. On 28 December 1978, the outgoing Geisel government authorized Eletrobras, the state-owned holding company of the federal and state power companies, to take over Light under the following conditions: Eletrobras accepted total responsibility for Light's debt of US $1,050 million, (of which 70% was foreign debts), and the Brazilian government paid compensation in foreign currency, totalling US $380 million, of which US$210 million, the equivalent of Light's invested and re-invested capital registered with the Banco Central, was paid immediately in cash, and the remaining US$170 million within 90 days.

The above conditions differed greatly from the few previous nationalizations in the early 1960s, when the outflow of foreign exchange was held to a minimum. In the case of the nationalization of the telephone utilities of CTB in Rio de Janeiro and Sao Paulo in 1965, for example, only 10% of the sum indemnified was paid in foreign exchange, in cash. The remaining 90% was split: 15% was paid in government bonds, payable in installments over 20 years, and the remaining 75% was to be entirely re-invested in Brazil. At that time an extensive public debate preceded the final negotiations. In the case of Light, however, the government behaved in an extremely highhanded manner – the nationalization was undertaken without any previous public debate or consultation with Congress, which was in recess at the time. Such public debate could have been expected to clarify, for example, whether commissions of US$38 million were paid to Antonio Galotti, Light's chief executive, as was suggested in the Brazilian weekly *Movimento* in July 1979. Moreover, it would have brought to the public's attention the global strategy of a foreign direct investor whose concessions, in this case, were due to run out at the end of the 1980s.

However, such considerations were not the concern of BRASCAN's shareholders, who 'greeted with enthusiasm' the happy outcome of a strategy which had been initiated in 1962, when they gave a broad authorization to the company 'to dispose of such concessions as opportunity and circumstances might permit'.[7] Meanwhile the management was able not only to dispose of BRASCAN's concessions in Light 'in the best interests of BRASCAN and its shareholders', as the company boasted in its 1978 annual report, but also to replace and multiply them.

The latter is worth emphasizing since, prior to 1967, BRASCAN had no significant investments in Canada, and almost all its interests were in Brazil, mainly in Light; at the end of 1978, on the other hand, BRASCAN reported an equity capital of US $190 million in Canada, and US$250 million in Brazil as registered foreign capital other than its former holdings in Light. Thus disposable funds were used for diversification rather than being channeled back into Light's expansion and maintenance programmes, which were funded via debt capital. Consequently, interest payments increased and the outlook for the transfer of profits and dividends abroad became gloomier after 1977, when, for the last time, the company transferred abroad US$29 million. Thereafter the snowball effect of debt capital caused a rapid decline in the rate of return on equity. Thus, at the end of 1978 when Light had definitely lost its capacity to serve as a 'cash cow' for BRASCAN's shareholders, the Brazilian government promptly announced the nationalization.

The above cases illustrate the objectives and methods of some foreign enterprises in Brazil. In order to maximize returns, foreign direct investors have centered on the growth sectors, become associated with the concentrated industries, and used their power to influence their bargaining relationship with successive governments in Brazil. The result has been a laissez-faire environment, in which the government has lost its capacity to be an unbiased, neutral 'regulator' between the objectives of foreign direct investors and the economic, social and political interests of the country.

Economic Growth – But For Whom?

Sesmaria is a Portuguese word, which literally means 'a land grant' and technically refers to the colonial period in Brazil when huge agricultural states were granted by the Portuguese Crown. During the 1970s, however, the idea of a new *Sesmaria* epoch has become increasingly widespread in Brazil, in particular with respect to the activities of giant foreign-owned agribusiness such as the Volkswagen or the JARI projects in the Amazon region. These projects, which are highly capital intensive, are mainly export-oriented. Like the *Sesmaria* some centuries ago they do little to promote the social integration of the regions they dominate. Is Brazil trying to return to the *Sesmaria* epoch? Is the Brazilian government ignoring the lessons of history in Brazil, by handing over the country's last and largest frontier, the Amazon region, to large foreign and local enterprises, thus creating export enclaves and allowing an unlimited exploitation of the land and people?

These questions might be regarded as inappropriate for a government whose objectives are similar to those of private enterprises, i.e. the maximization of output. There is no doubt that the country's economy needs to grow in order to provide employment opportunities for its 40 million strong workforce, which increases yearly by over 1½ million. Given this, the questions arise as to which sectors should grow, for whom and how such growth should be achieved? Industry has grown most rapidly in recent years, and within industry the fastest growing sectors have been those in which foreign direct investors have been most concentrated. In the 1980s a shift of emphasis is being predicted toward agro-industry. However, the objective is not to promote agricultural production in order to grow food for the country's largely under-nourished population; rather the two major aims are to promote both exports and the agro-chemical industry, which will produce alternatives to petrol. These developments will integrate one of the most reactionary forces in Brazil, the landed oligarchy, into the heart of the Brazilian economy.

The realization of both these objectives should allow the present economic model to continue to expand. They should compensate for such constraints as increases in oil prices, the restricted internal market due to greater concentration of personal income, the growth of the country's foreign debt, and inflation. In other worlds these objectives should help to maintain an economic model in which markets are imperfect, governments are closely linked with the interests of the international business community, and in which benefits accrue to a minority to the detriment of the country's largely impoverished majority.

The increasing concentration of personal income was illustrated in a survey on Brazil published by the *Economist* in August 1979. Despite considerable growth rates mainly during the Kubitschek government and Delfim Neto's first period as Brazil's 'overlord' (1967-74), personal income was further concentrated among the richest 5% of the economically active population to the disadvantage of the poorest 50%. In 1960 the latter group received 17.7% of total personal income, but only 11.8% in 1977. This trend is hardly surprising if one takes into account the fact that a great variety of tactics were being employed to keep wages as low as possible. In 1973, for example, the general price index, which has been an important factor in determining annual (now six-monthly) wage increases, was 'artificially', to use the *Economist's* term, reduced from 27% to 15½%.

Another consequence of Brazil's growth strategy has been an increase in the foreign debt. At the end of 1979 it was the world's largest and amounted to roughly US$50 billion, a figure more than three times higher than that year's earnings from exports. Interest alone is causing a snowball effect. In the period from 1972 to 1978 interest payments increased over six times, from US$360 million in 1972 to US$2,580 million in 1978. Finally it is worth emphasising that in 1979 inflation was 77%.

The increasing exploitation in Brazil has strengthened the will of the labour force to organize itself. The strikes of the late 1970s were an early expression of labour's reaction. Furthermore, in 1979 a partial political amnesty allowed political leaders such as governor Miguel Arraes of Pernambuco and the federal deputy Alencar Furtado, who presided over the congressional hearings on the multinationals in 1976, to return to the political stage. These leaders fully recognize that, in the long run, solutions to Brazil's economic, social and political problems call for a reorientation of the country's priorities. Such a reorientation, however, would require the government in Brazil to pursue different objectives from those which suit foreign enterprises. This conflict of interests may be resolved either by negotiation or adaptation or by open struggle.

Foreign direct investors still seem confident that the distribution of power is in their favour. The massive inflow over the last years of the 1970s has proven this. Schliemann confirmed their confidence, as shown in Table 3, which presents the percentage of British and German parent companies which considered factors such as growth potential, political stability, etc. in Brazil to have improved, remained unchanged or worsened during the period 1973-78.[8]

Table 3 shows that both the British and the German companies judged the market growth potential and the political stability to have on balance improved. Of the 24 German parent

Table 3 — Foreign Direct Investors' Opinions Concerning Changes in Brazil During 1973-1978
(percentages)

Factor	United Kingdom (N=18)			Balance (+/-)	West Germany (N=24)			Balance (+/-)
	(+)	(=)	(-)		(+)	(=)	(-)	
Market growth potential	44	28	28	+16	39	39	22	+17
Political stability	17	72	11	+6	17	83	–	+17
Profit expectation	45	22	33	+12	9	32	59	-50
Profit remittance	–	89	11	-11	14	41	45	-31
Labour costs	6	39	55	-51	30	17	53	-23
Brazil's economic growth	17	28	55	-38	30	17	53	-23
Import restrictions	–	6	94	-94	–	9	91	-91
Prices of raw material	–	29	71	-71	–	17	83	-83
Finance possibilities in Brazil	22	39	39	-17	34	20	56	-22

Source: Schliemann (1979); answers to the question: From your point of view, how have each of the factors below changed in Brazil, for your company, over the last five years? Please tick for each row if (+) improved, (=) unchanged, or (-) worsened.

58

companies, which together employed 80,400 people in their largest subsidiaries in Brazil in 1976, *none considered that political stability had worsened in Brazil.* A further aspect worth emphasizing is profit expectations, in which the two countries diverge markedly. On balance 50% of the Germans thought the profit expectation to have worsened, in contrast to 12% of the British, for whom this factor was felt to have improved. The answers of the German firms were strongly influenced by the representatives of the automobile industry, and were, in addition, consistent with their future plans to invest more heavily in North America, given that country's market growth for German passenger cars as well as the then favourable US dollar-Deutschmark exchange trend. On the other hand, the answers of the British are only understandable if one takes into account the oligopolistic market structure with which foreign enterprises are associated and in which they can transfer increasing costs for labour, raw material, etc. to the consumer.

Events since 1978 have so far supported the confidence of foreign direct investors in Brazil. In early 1979 the outgoing Geisel government (1974-79) showed its clear subordination to the demands of foreign companies by its handling of the nationalization of Light. Moreover, in the present Figueiredo government Delfim Neto has regained the crucial position of planning minister after a short term in 1979 as minister of agriculture. Although his international open-door policy may have to be compromised to agree with the pro-American line of General Golbery who remains head of the President's civil household, and Heitor Aquino Ferreira, a former head of the JARI project and private secretary of both Presidents Geisel and Figueiredo, the main priorities (promotion of exports and agribusiness) still fit in with the objectives of foreign direct investors.

To use the words of Roberto Campos, Brazil's ambassador in London, writing on the 93rd birthday of Professor Eugenio Gudin, father of the Brazilian 'internationalist' school, whom he greatly admires: *'Nihil Novum Sub Sole'* (nothing new under the sun), the platform of President Figueiredo was already written by Professor Gudin 20 years ago'. Indeed, the package announced in December 1979 by President Figueiredo fully confirms Campos' statement. The cruzeiro had been devalued, import controls and export subsidies have been eliminated and economic neo-liberalism is once again the guiding principle of economic policy-making —

a process the Figueiredo government calls 'economic war'. However, one major question still remains: will these measures not in fact both fuel social conflict and increase economic constraints within Brazil?

(The author wishes to thank Mr Klaus Haberich for his many helpful comments.)

Footnotes

1. Connor, J.M. and Mueller, W.F., *Market Power and Profitability of Multinational Corporations in Brazil and Mexico,* Report to Subcommittee on Foreign Economic Policy of the Committee on Foreign Relations, United States Senate, US Government Printing Office: Washington, 1977.
2. Schliemann, P-U., *British and German Direct Investments in Brazil,* Institut fuer Iberoamerika-Kunde: Hamburg, 1979.
3. Diario do Congresso Nacional, *Relatorio e as Conclusoes da Comissao Parlamentar de Inquerito para Investigar o Comportamento e as influencias das Empresas Multinacionais e do Capital Estrangeiro no Brasil,* Camara dos Deputados, Suplemento do No.79, 1 de julho 1976: Brasilia.
4. Newfarmer, R., 'Oligopolistic Tactics to Control Markets and the Growth of TNCs in Brazil's Electrical Industry', *The Drama of Development Studies,* Vol.15, April 1979: London.
5. Diario do Congresso Nacional (1976), *op.cit.*
6. Diario do Congresso Nacional, *Conclusoes da Comissao Parlamentar de Inquerito Destinada a Investigar o Custo do Veiculo Nacional,* Camara dos Deputados, Suplemento ao No.130, 13 de outubro 1970: Brasilia.
7. BRASCAN report, June 1979 and *Financial Times,* 29.12.1978.
8. Schliemann, *op.cit.*

EUROPE AND LATIN AMERICA: THE NUCLEAR CONNECTION
JEAN CARRIERE

The nuclear policies of states on the threshold of becoming nuclear powers, such as Argentina, raise a number of important issues, not the least of which is the role played by West Germany in supporting the development of a nuclear industry with military potential in Latin America.

This article will describe the nuclear development programmes of Brazil and Argentina and, with particular reference to the former, will examine critically West Germany's involvement in these programmes. It will also discuss the military potential of these programmes and several issues which are central to the proliferation debate, namely: Brazil and Agentina's attitudes to the non-proliferation treaty, the factors likely to induce one or both countries to acquire nuclear weapons and the specific risks associated with the development of a large scale nuclear industry by semi-industrialized, periphery capitalist countries such as the two under consideration.

The Argentine Programme

Small research reactors have been operating in Argentina for over twenty years, but Latin America really entered the nuclear age in 1974 when the sub-continent's first power reactor was switched on at Atucha, near Buenos Aires, and began to feed into the regional grid.

The Atucha reactor had been in the planning stages since the mid-1960s, when Argentina decided to base its entire nuclear development programme on the natural uranium/heavy water cycle. It was known that this decision would cost the country a great deal of money since reactors based on this cycle are technologically more complex and more expensive to build than the light water reactors. However, there were a number of advantages in choosing the natural uranium/heavy water cycle, in particular the fact that these reactors are fuelled by natural uranium — readily found and mined in Argentina — and not by enriched uranium which can only be obtained at the discretion of the advanced nuclear countries. Thus Argentina opted for self reliance in fuel supply.

The first plant was built by the German firm Siemens and has a capacity of 320 megawatts (MW). A second plant with almost double that capacity (600 MW), again based on the natural uranium cycle, is now under construction and is scheduled to come into operation either in late 1980 or early 1981. The contract for a third plant, this time of 700 MW, was signed with the German firm KWU in October 1979; this plant is scheduled to go into operation in the mid-1980s.

Three other points are worth noting in relation to the Argentine nuclear programme:

— high quality weapons-grade plutonium can be made, given appropriate fuel reprocessing facilities, from the Argentine reactors, although at considerable cost;

— such a fuel reprocessing facility — albeit a small experimental one — is due to open in 1980 and, in the words of an Argentine government communique issued in London in February 1979, 'it will give us, one supposes, the ability to build nuclear bombs':

— self-reliance with respect to fuel reprocessing will soon be followed by self-reliance in the heavy water needed to moderate the power reactors, as in March 1980 Argentina signed a contract with a Swiss firm, Sulzer Brothers, for the construction of a heavy water plant with a capacity of 250 tons a year, sufficient to satisfy the heavy water requirements of the country's nuclear plants for years to come.

All this means that Argentina may now have the capacity to manufacture nuclear weapons, and that by the mid-1980s at the latest the country will control the entire nuclear cycle leading to and including the capacity to make weapons-grade plutonium.

The Brazilian Programme

The Brazilian nuclear programme is more recent and still depends on the successful implementation of the so-called nuclear 'deal of the century', an umbrella agreement signed between Brazil and West Germany in 1975 and worth approximately US$5 billion in export orders for the German nuclear industry.

Since the agreement was signed, there has hardly been a month when the specialist nuclear press has not commented on the deal. This is understandable as it is by far the largest nuclear sales contract ever agreed to: eight power reactors, a uranium enrichment plant and a fuel reprocessing plant, all to be constructed before 1990.

However, the Brazilian programme has been very slow in getting off the ground. The first nuclear power plant, built by the American firm Westinghouse, will provide 650 MW and should go into operation in 1980 after years of delay due to engineering and other difficulties. The first of the German plants under the agreement described above, has been under construction almost from the time the agreement was signed, but work has been delayed by a host of engineering problems, including shifting the entire site on which the plant is being built. Inauguration, originally scheduled for 1978, has now been postponed until the mid-1980s. Only one other plant of the eight provided for by the agreement, is likely to be completed before 1990. Nevertheless, it is still likely that within the next ten years Brazil will have two, perhaps three, functioning power plants as well as a small uranium enrichment facility enabling it to produce weapons-grade uranium if it so wishes. The programme will not be as ambitious as was originally conceived, but its military potential will still be there.

Thus, both Brazil and Argentina will probably have acquired the capability of making nuclear weapons without external assistance or supplies well before the end of the decade. There is no certainty that either country will want to make use of this capacity, but the option will be theirs.

West German Involvement

West Germany has been involved in the nuclear programmes of both Argentina and Brazil, but the agreement with Brazil deserves special study because it shows how competition for nuclear contacts between American and a major European supplier has led to steps that could have extremely serious consequences for nuclear weapons proliferation.

It is not the size of the West German-Brazil agreement which is its most controversial feature but the fact that for the first time the full nuclear cycle, including uranium enrichment and fuel reprocessing facilities, has been provided to a non-nuclear weapons state as part of a package, thus giving the nuclear programme of the purchasing country a clear military potential. Until 1975, none of the nuclear weapons states had agreed to the sale of enrichment and reprocessing technology precisely because of the implications for nuclear weapons proliferation. Germany was the first supplier country to break ranks, in spite of strong United States pressure not to do so.

Perhaps the most disturbing aspect of the agreement was the inclusion of a fuel reprocessing plant which makes it possible to recycle nuclear fuel and produces plutonium as a by-product. Such a plant is not commercially viable when used to recycle fuel for power reactors. It only makes sense as a means of producing plutonium for the purpose of manufacturing nuclear weapons, and only nuclear weapons states such as the Unites States operate them, as part of their nuclear weapons programme. Why then did Brazil insist that the package include the reprocessing facilities, and why did West Germany agree to supply it?

The answer to the first question is still shrouded in military secrecy. As for the second question, there is strong evidence that Germany's motives were primarily commercial, and that the Germans agreed to supply the more controversial technology only at Brazil's insistence and under the threat of losing the entire package.

By the early 1970s, Germany's reactor manufacturers were in deep trouble at home. Not only was the industry operating with a high level of overcapacity – around 35% – but its prospects for the future were bleak. A drop in electricity consumption, the availability of surplus coal and oil, and the increasing ability of the anti-nuclear movement to hold up nuclear projects in the courts, all contributed to the industry's despondency. One response was a vigorous export drive, and German nuclear salesmen travelled the globe looking for customers, prepared to make unprecedented concessions in order to secure agreements. There is little doubt that in this kind of climate, the enrichment reprocessing technology was offered as the Germans' trump card, one which competing US firms operating under the handicap of a US government ban on such exports were unable to match. Thus, in order to protect its nuclear industry from a prolonged slump, and without consulting its nuclear allies nor even bringing this issue into the political arena in Germany, the German government concluded an agreement that could have far-reaching consequences for the way in which nuclear suppliers and threshold states deal with each other, both bilaterally and within the multilateral system represented by the non-proliferation treaty. The next section will examine Argentine and Brazilian attitudes to the question of nuclear arms, specifically to the Non-Proliferation Treaty of 1970 (NPT).

The Non-Proliferation Treaty

To understand the position of Argentina and Brazil vis-a-vis the NPT, it is essential to begin with the distinction, rarely emphasized by the superpowers, between horizontal and vertical proliferation. Horizontal proliferation corresponds to the spread of nuclear weapons, and the capacity to deliver them to distant targets, from one state to another, i.e. proliferation occurs when non-nuclear weapons states come to possess and control the use of nuclear weapons. Vertical proliferation refers to the manufacture by nuclear weapons states of an ever increasing number of nuclear weapons, or of new and more dangerous types of weapons and delivery systems.

The NPT addresses itself almost exclusively to the problem of horizontal proliferation. Most nuclear threshold states, including Argentina and Brazil, have argued that because the NPT fails to deal with both, equally dangerous, forms of weapons proliferation, it is a discriminatory agreement and an ineffective approach to the problem of controlling the spread of nuclear weapons.

On the basis of this argument, Argentina and Brazil have refused to become parties to the NPT. Because of its discriminatory nature, they argue, the NPT would have the effect of limiting the development of non-nuclear states, while doing nothing to prevent nuclear states from consolidating their lead in a field which has crucial scientific, technological, commercial and security dimensions.

There are a number of other arguments put forward against the NPT: it maintains the present international and regional balance of power; it offers inadequate security guarantees to non-nuclear states that are party to it; it contains almost no provisions for sharing the benefits of nuclear technology; and finally, the NPT fails to link the issue of weapons proliferation to the question of nuclear disarmament, so that no formal disarmament agreement exists to put pressure on the nuclear weapons states in the same way that the non-proliferation agreement is designed to place constraints on the policies of non-nuclear weapons states.

For all these reasons, both Brazil and Argentina have rejected the NPT and claim the right to autonomy in decision making on all matters relating to nuclear technology.

Two main points should be noted in relation to Argentine and Brazilian attitudes to non-proliferation. First, the arguments put forward by Argentina and Brazil suggest they still claim the right to exercize the option of acquiring nuclear weapons. What factors might influence a decision on that option and what are the specific risks associated with the development of nuclear weapons by these two particular states?

Secondly, these governments' critique of the NPT does point to some serious weaknesses in the way the superpowers have handled the issue of proliferation since the NPT discussions began in 1968. We should therefore look at the proposals that have been put forward to control nuclear proliferation in a manner more likely to accommodate the objectives and elicit the support of nuclear threshold states such as Argentina and Brazil.

Motivations for Acquiring Nuclear Weapons

Argentina and Brazil are not among the nuclear threshold states most likely to want to acquire nuclear weapons in the immediate future. Nevertheless, while regional tensions in Latin America fall short of the level that might lead to a regional arms race, there is an historic rivalry between Brazil and Argentina that could threaten regional stability in the future. Brazil maintains she is entitled to regional hegemony by virtue of her size and geographical dominance of the region, while Argentina resists all attempts by Brazil to consolidate that dominance. There are a number of longstanding conflicts between the two countries, such as Argentina's claims to Antarctica, and the use of the Parana river for the Itaipu hydroelectric project. Serious trouble could erupt if Brazil and Argentina supported different political factions in a in a neighbouring state during a crisis of succession.

These issues are unlikely to result in open warfare between the two regional powers, but there are enough issues simmering to maintain a climate of rivalry and mutual suspicion, which will encourage hard line defence postures as a precaution against future conflict. It is in this climate that nuclear decision-making will take place during the next ten or fifteen years.

From Brazil's point of view, it is difficult to imagine what advantages might be gained in terms of its regional domination from the acquisition — and one supposes the testing - of nuclear weapons. If the pro-weapons lobby gains greater influence in the years to come and Brazil edges towards a decision to produce and test nuclear bombs, it will not be the result of concern for her place in the regional system, but from a belief in Brazil's destiny as an international power. Clearly, part of the foreign and defence policy establishment believes that Brazil will only fulfil its destiny in world politics if it exercizes its nuclear option as a way of ensuring that its claims are taken seriously.

With respect to Argentina, there is a widespread belief among students of Latin American politics that parts of her armed forces are under the spell of the nuclear weapons option, which they see as the logical outcome of the country's long standing effort to build up a strong nuclear research establishment and a self-reliant nuclear power industry. Given the irreversible gap in population, resources, armed forces and industrial weight between Argentina and Brazil, Argentina may very well see the acquisition of nuclear weapons as 'the great equalizer' which, by a single gesture, would redress the power balance between the two dominant nations of the sub-continent. Brazil would then feel compelled to develop nuclear arms of its own if it had not already done so, but mutual nuclear deterrence at the regional level would necessarily favour the weaker of the two states.

There are other possible, perhaps more likely scenarios. One or both countries could choose the Israeli route of taking steps to manufacture nuclear weapons but stopping just short of final assembly and testing (some observers believe that Israel is no more than 24 hours away from having an operational nuclear weapon, yet it is spared the political costs of being identified as a 'proliferator'). Or again, both sides could reluctantly decide in favour of the weapons option as a result of incorrect perception of each other's intentions.

Thus, while Argentina and Brazil have not so far openly expressed the intention of acquiring nuclear weapons, it is by no means certain that one or both of them will not do so during the years to come. Any one of the factors mentioned earlier could lead to tensions that would sharpen the rivalry between the two countries and possibly strengthen the position of the nuclear lobbies. If, therefore, it is well within the realm of possibilities that these countries will join the nuclear club, it is legitimate to ask what specific risks such a turn of events might carry.

The Question of Political Instability

Horizontal proliferation is regarded as highly dangerous for world peace, not only because it means that more countries will be in a position to detonate nuclear explosions but also because some of the present threshold states have a potentially violent and unstable political future. It is argued — I believe with some justification — that nuclear weapons in the hands of politically unstable states would represent a far greater threat to world peace than the same weapons under the control of politically stable states.

There are two potential dangers involved. First, a ruling group or class under threat of being swept from power might embark upon an adventurist foreign policy in the hope of diverting attention from the internal political strains, and thus increase the risk of war. Secondly, the foreign policy of a politically unstable state is often unpredictable and subject to sudden shifts. As a result, neighbouring states may incorrectly read the unstable state's foreign policy objectives, thus possibly provoking an unwanted war.

There are, at present, good reasons to believe that Argentina and Brazil will experience profound political instability during the coming years. It is not assumed that they will be unstable in the future merely because they have been unstable in the past. For one thing such an assumption would not be valid for Brazil which, except for a few very brief crises of succession, has had a stable authoritarian regime, since the mid-1960s.

The argument rests on other grounds. In order to appreciate the strains that are likely to build up during the years to come, we must understand the development strategies pursued by Brazil since the mid-1960s and by Argentina since the mid-1970s. Although there are many important differences between them, they share certain key features, have the same internal logic and are likely to produce comparable political tensions.

68

The key features of this development strategy are, first of all, an attempt to achieve rapid industrial growth and the modernization of the productive apparatus; secondly a systematic effort rapidly to increase the rate of capital accumulation in order to fuel that growth; and thirdly, a no less systematic attack on working class standards of living and on the labour movement as a whole in order to concentrate incomes and open the way for that high rate of accumulation.

It is clear that the major source of political tension most likely to lead to great political instability is the sharp deterioration in working class living standards and the violent repression of workers and their organizations. Evidence of the sharp decline in living standards is now overwhelming. For example, Brazilian families on the minimum wage must now work almost twice the number of hours they worked in 1965 to sustain themselves at a basic minimum level of consumption. In Argentina the real purchasing power of wages has dropped by more than half between 1970 and 1977. The important thing about working class consumption in both countries is not so much that it is low but that it has moved rapidly downwards after a period of *relative* well being. It is important to note that the idea of a downturn in working class fortunes is a key element of most theories of mass mobilization and revolution.

The other element of the two regimes' labour control strategies which is almost certain to lead to a build up of political tensions is, in the case of Argentina, the direct repression of workers and their organizations. This aspect has been well documented by such organizations as Amnesty International and other international bodies concerned with human rights. Workers and trade union leaders have disappeared without trace, hundreds fill the prisons, thousands of others are in exile, most of them because they threatened the state's control of trade union activities. In the case of Brazil, official violence against the workers has been less widespread in recent years, but the state still manages effectively to control the working class movement through a corporatist system of labour institutions inherited from the presidency of Vargas in the 1940s. In both countries, workers are showing greater militancy in their protests against falling living standards and the government-imposed straight jacket on the labour movement. Hundreds of thousands of workers have been involved in recent strikes in key industrial sectors in Brazil, such as the metal workers strike. In Argentina, labour protest and discontent is continuous, though not on such a large scale, in spite of the threat of long jail sentences for what would be regarded in most industrial countries as legitimate trade union activity.

Societies where the type of development strategies summarized earlier are being applied frequently exhibit deep contradictions that are likely to result in serious political instability. The logic of accumulation in periphery capitalist countries *requires* income concentration, a fall in the standard of living of the working class and a repressive state to enforce it. At the same time, industrial growth produced an expanded and more concentrated urban working class whose economic and political demands become more insistent and strident, and which the system is unable to meet without sabotaging its entire economic programme. There is a rich literature on the economic and political contradictions that are specific to periphery capitalist societies, and much of it warns of latent class antagonisms erupting into violent political upheavals in the years to come. It would be nonsense to argue that these contradictions are unfolding in a mechanical and clearly predictable manner, but at the same time it would be irresponsible to ignore them and the high risks of internal conflict to which they give rise.

Controlling Proliferation

Brazil and Argentina have acquired nuclear cycles that will enable them to manufacture nuclear weapons well before the decade is out. Should either of them decide to do so, the risks associated with proliferation of any kind would be aggravated by the likelihood of serious internal political conflict and intra-regional tensions during the coming years. How can these risks be minimized?

It is now too late to prevent either country from manufacturing nuclear weapons on a small scale, if that is what they wish to do. However it might be possible for the nuclear weapons states to dampen the motivation of the non-nuclear weapons states to develop the kinds of energy programmes that are consistent with production of nuclear weapons on a larger scale, by altering the terms of the debate on nuclear proliferation.

In the first place, the nuclear weapons states should recognize that their credibility as opponents of proliferation is seriously undermined by their inability to reduce vertical proliferation — the development by these states of new and ever more dangerous weapons systems — to any significant extent. Until now, proliferation has been treated as a separate issue to disarmament. This compartmentalization of issues that are closely related, and the slow pace of disarmament negotiations, are seen by the threshold states as symbolic of the nuclear weapons states' unwillingness to deal with vertical proliferation issues and hence have contributed to the threshold states' suspicion of nuclear weapons states' anti-proliferation doctrines.

Secondly, threshold states will rarely be deterred from pursuing a policy of nuclear autonomy, which means access to the means of producing nuclear weapons, until they can receive absolute guarantee of continuity of nuclear fuel supply as well as the certainty that rival states are not acquiring weapons-grade fissionable material to which they are denied access.

This opens up a very large question which is likely to loom even larger during the coming decade, that of international control of the means of producing nuclear fuel and weapons-grade fissionable material on a large scale. However utopian this may seem at this stage, the nuclear weapons states will have to consider the possibility of placing all of their enrichment and reprocessing facilities under the authority of international supervisory bodies with full participation by the threshold states. Obviously there is no space here to examine the implications of such a far-reaching proposal except to say that without a solution of this type it is difficult to see how the threshold states' legitimate demands for a secure, non-discretionary system of fuel allocation and for assurances that weapons-grade material is not falling into the hands of rival states can ever be met.

Clearly these two enormously complex and high controversial proposals that are floated in various forms from time to time are meant to deal with the problem of proliferation over the long term. In the meantime some shorter term measures are needed in order to buy time for the longer term approaches to produce results. And the most effective way of buying time is to follow the American lead and freeze all exports of enrichment and reprocessing facilities. On this question Europe has vacillated and Germany has broken ranks, succumbing to the pressures from its nuclear industry. It is up to the anti-nuclear movements in Europe to ensure that it does not happen again.

Editor's note: As the review was going to press an agreement between Brazil and Argentina was announced providing for future cooperation on nuclear technology for peaceful purposes. However, no further details are available.

APPENDICES

APPENDICES

Notes

Appendix 1 – Trade

Table 1: EEC/Latin America (principal trading partners) Imports
    1a: EEC/Latin America (other trading partners) Imports
    2: EEC/Latin America (principal trading partners) Exports
    2a: EEC/Latin America (other trading partners) Exports
    3: EEC/Latin America Trade by Principal Product Groups
    4: UK, EEC, US and Japanese Trade with Latin America

The data on UK, EEC, US and Japanese trade with Latin America are included for comparative purposes. Comprehensive import/export data between individual Latin American and EEC countries are available in OECD and/or EEC official annual/monthly trade publications. Past and present copies of all these documents can be found in the Statistics and Market Intelligence Library, Department of Industry, Export House, 50 Ludgate Hill, London EC4.

Appendix 2 – Investment

Table 1: Total Flows of Resources to Latin America (excluding aid)
    2: British Investment in Latin America
    3: Stocks of Direct Investment in Latin America, Selected Countries

Table 1 shows the total recorded net flows of resources, including direct investment but excluding aid, to individual Latin American countries. However, the only readily available general source for such data, the OECD annual review on overseas development cooperation, has this information almost entirely in aggregate form and it has thus not been possible to identify the flows from specific countries or the EEC. Tables 2 and 3 may serve to indicate some aspects of this information.

Appendix 3 – Aid

Table 1: Receipts by Latin America of Development Assistance
    2: British Aid to Latin America
    3: Disbursements of Development Assistance from EEC Countries

Table 1 shows the net receipts by individual Latin American countries of bilateral and multilateral development assistance. The source, the OECD annual review of overseas development cooperation, is the same as for Appendix 2 and the same difficulty applies regarding the lack of disaggregated information. It has therefore not been possible to identify the net contribution to Latin America from specific countries or the EEC. Tables 2 and 3 may serve to indicate some aspects of this information. It is clear, at least, that aid to Latin America does not form a significant proportion of the EEC's overall commitments.

Appendix 4 – Arms Sales

The information in this appendix covers only major weapons. Details of sales of small arms, ammunition, police equipment, etc, are not readily available. Data on major arms agreements between Latin American countries and non-European countries are also included for comparative purposes. The Latin America Bureau's 1979 annual review of British-Latin American relations, *Britain and Latin America*, contains comprehensive tables covering all aspects of Latin America and the arms trade drawn from a special report by the Stockholm International Peace Research Institute in *World Armaments and Disarmament, SIPRI Yearbook 1978*.

Sources

Most of the above tables have been computed from the most recent data available in the sources listed and have not, therefore, been extracted directly. For cross-checking please refer to the notes given at the foot of each table.

Official British government statistics on Overseas Transactions (Business Monitor series) has recently (1977) dropped specific mention of individual Latin American countries although Aid Statistics (1979) are still reasonably comprehensive. This documentation is also available in the Statistics and Market Intelligence Library, Department of Industry.

Appendix 1 — Trade

Table 1 — Total EEC Imports from Latin America (cif)

US$ million	1974	1975	1976	1977	1978	1979 (1st 3 qrtrs)	Some proportions 1975	1977	1979
Argentina	1555	1066	1477	2098	2550	2093	13.2%	18.5%	18.4%
Brazil	2675	2713	2982	3940	3905	3606	33.6%	34.8%	31.8%
Chile	798	631	767	751	929	1074	7.8%	6.6%	9.5%
Colombia	373	497	623	811	1034	798	6.2%	7.2%	7.0%
Cuba	110	89	139	126	161	167	1.1%	1.1%	1.5%
Ecuador	138	139	134	212	218	155	1.7%	1.9%	1.4%
Mexico	412	385	415	496	498	434	4.8%	4.4%	3.8%
Panama	74	115	114	149	134	128	1.4%	1.3%	1.1%
Peru	425	323	331	343	338	398	4.0%	3.0%	3.5%
Venezuela	906	961	908	584	749	902	11.9%	5.2%	7.9%
Other Latin America[1]	962	1147	1232	1811	1658	1600	14.3%	16.0%	14.1%
Total	8428	8066	9122	11321	12174	11355	100.0%	100.0%	100.0%
Latin America as % of all countries	2.9	2.7	2.9	2.9	2.6	2.7			
Latin America as % of developing countries[2]	11.6	12.0	11.7	13.1	13.4	13.5			

Source: OECD Statistics of Foreign Trade, Janaury 1980

1. Bolivia, Costa Rica, Dominican Republic, El Salvador, Guatemala, Haiti, Honduras, Nicaragua, Paraguay, Uruguay. Some information on EEC imports from these countries may be found in Table 1a.
2. Developing countries are defined as all countries with the exception of OECD countries, centrally planned economies (including Yugoslavia) and South Africa. Figures for 'unspecified' trade are excluded.

Table 1a – Total EEC Imports from Other Latin American Countries (cif)

US$ million	1965	1970	1973	1977	1978
Bolivia	56	96	88	152	130
Costa Rica	28	51	120	202	219
Dominican Republic	16	18	60	62	67
El Salvador	67	69	73	379	216
Guatemala	51	59	91	291	268
Haiti	18	14	19	54	56
Honduras	23	47	61	128	137
Nicaragua	43	32	59	184	154
Paraguay	23	27	83	151	172
Uruguay	102	88	161	209	240
Total[1]	427	501	815	1812	1659

Source: *Statistiques sur les Echanges Commerciaux de la Communaute Euro-peene et des Autres Pays Industrialises Occidentaux avec l'Amerique Latine 1965-1978*, Statistics Office of the European Community, December 1979.

1. See also Note 1 of Table 1. The two different sources used in the compilation of Tables 1 and 1a account for minor discrepancies in the figures.

Table 2a: Total EEC Exports to Other Latin American Countries (fob)

US$ million	1965	1970	1973	1977	1978
Bolivia	28	36	32	120	147
Costa Rica	37	50	72	107	137
Dominican Republic	20	51	68	92	94
El Salvador	40	40	58	115	133
Guatemala	45	50	72	165	196
Haiti	8	15	27	39	44
Honduras	14	20	29	54	70
Nicaragua	37	31	48	85	68
Paraguay	18	19	24	63	88
Uruguay	44	68	54	132	170
Total[1]	291	380	484	972	1147

Source: *Statistiques sur les Echanges Commerciaux de la Communaute Europeene et des Autres Pays Industrialises Occidentaux avec l'Amerique Latine 1965-1978*, Statistics Office of the European Community, December 1979.

1. See also Note 1 of Table 2. The two different sources used in the compilation of Tables 2 and 2a account for minor discrepancies in the figures.

Table 2: Total EEC Exports to Latin America (fob)

US$ million	1974	1975	1976	1977	1978	1979 (1st 3 qrtrs)	Some proportions 1975	1977	1979
Argentina	989	1001	810	1148	1399	1522	10.4%	11.3%	15.1%
Brazil	3126	2870	2472	2503	2696	2334	29.9%	24.7%	23.2%
Chile	338	295	257	346	443	465	3.1%	3.4%	4.6%
Columbia	376	386	346	497	557	518	4.0%	4.9%	5.1%
Cuba	421	548	419	391	310	252	5.7%	3.9%	2.5%
Ecuador	179	190	198	370	425	355	2.0%	3.6%	3.5%
Mexico	1112	1206	1084	914	1633	1495	12.6%	9.0%	14.9%
Panama	259	421	413	275	334	285	4.4%	2.7%	2.8%
Peru	418	630	386	335	325	533	6.6%	3.3%	5.3%
Venezuela	954	1337	1523	2402	2376	1396	13.9%	23.7%	13.9%
Other Latin America[1]	738	721	744	971	1159	911	7.4%	9.5%	9.1%
Total	8910	9605	8652	10152	11657	10066	100.0%	100.0%	100.0%
Latin America as % of all countries	3.3	3.3	2.7	2.7	2.6	2.5			
Latin America as % of developing countries[2]	21.2	17.6	15.1	14.3	13.7	14.8			

Source: OECD, *Statistics of Foreign Trade*, January 1980

1. Bolivia, Costa Rica, Dominican Republic, El Salvador, Guatemala, Haiti, Honduras, Nicaragua, Paraguay, Uruguay. Some information on EEC exports to these countries may be found in Table 2.
2. Developing countries as defined in Note 2, Table 1.

Table 3: EEC Trade with Latin America for 1977-78 by
Principal Product Groups

EEC Imports (cif) from Latin America

	Value US$ million		% of Total	
	1977	1978	1977	1978
Meat and Fish	393	450	3.5	3.7
Maize and Other Cereal	325	241	2.9	2.0
Other Food Stuffs	2148	2272	19.0	18.7
Beverages and Tobacco	3116	2781	27.5	22.9
Wool, Cotton and Prod.	584	617	5.2	5.1
Clothes, Furs, and Leather	338	351	3.0	2.9
Wood and Pulp	119	147	1.1	1.2
Metals (raw)	1641	1740	14.5	14.3
Petroleum/Oil	319	342	2.8	2.8
Machinery and Transport	137	209	1.2	1.7
'Other'	2199	3005	19.4	24.7
Total	11319	12155	100.0	100.0

EEC Exports (fob) to Latin America

	Value US$ million		% of Total	
	1977	1978	1977	1978
Raw Materials	768	910	7.6	7.9
Chemical Products	1720	2055	17.1	17.8
Manufactured Goods	1412	1955	14.0	16.9
Machinery:				
Non-Electrical	3022	3312	30.0	28.7
Electrical	1128	1216	11.2	10.5
Transport and Materials	1322	1373	13.1	11.9
'Other'	713	727	7.0	6.3
Total	10085	11548	100.0	100.0

Source: *Statistiques sur les Echanges Commerciaux de la Communaute Euro-
peene et des Autres Pays Industrialises Occidentaux avec l'Amerique Latine
1965-1978*, Statistics Office of the European Community, December 1979.

Table 4: UK, EEC, US and Japanese Imports (cif) from and Exports (fob) to Latin America. First three quarters of 1979

US$ million	UK		EEC		USA		JAPAN	
	Imports from	Exports to	Imports from	Exports to	Imports from	Exports to	Imports from	Exports to
Argentina	236	187	2093	1422	466	1164	358	314
Brazil	655	417	3606	2334	2304	2378	884	830
Chile	231	63	1074	465	324	604	377	166
Colombia	41	83	798	518	883	1006	117	261
Cuba	25	62	167	252	0	0	111	119
Ecuador	10	52	155	355	586	502	29	142
Mexico	51	206	434	1495	6161	6916	324	586
Panama	7	38	128	285	137	371	161	621
Peru	95	36	398	533	746	500	358	99
Venezuela	139	223	902	1396	3762	2868	91	574
Other Latin America	116	168	1600	911	2330	2127	326	497
Total	1606	1535	11355	10066	17699	18436	3136	4209
Latin America as % of all countries	2.2	2.4	2.7	2.5	11.9	14.2	4.0	5.7
Latin America as % of all developing countries[1]	12.3	10.6	13.5	14.8	27.1	40.8	7.4	12.7

Source: OECD, *Statistics of Foreign Trade*, January 1980

1. Developing countries as previously defined.

Appendix 2 — Investment

Table 1: Total Recorded Net Flow of Resources to Latin America from DAC Countries *Less* ODA. 1975-78[1]

US$ million	1975	1976	1977	1978
Argentina	306.4	487.5	344.4	1085.0
Uruguay	46.0	33.8	4.0	2.4
Paraguay	7.6	23.3	23.2	24.9
Brazil	2534.8	3628.9	2168.1	4543.1
Bolivia	45.3	49.0	76.5	85.1
Chile	-355.5	-69.1	-136.3	118.4
Peru	501.1	276.8	202.2	280.6
Ecuador	-0.9	65.2	132.4	320.2
Venezuela	520.1	-339.9	794.0	1415.5
Colombia	159.9	175.9	181.6	255.5
Mexico	1320.1	1236.0	1797.7	2485.4
Panama	588.8	297.6	530.0	540.5
Costa Rica	17.7	40.3	69.8	59.0
Nicaragua	31.8	28.0	19.5	6.8
Honduras	10.5	20.8	26.2	15.9
El Salvador	34.1	11.9	-0.2	32.4
Guatemala	11.8	33.3	72.2	80.5
Dominican Republic	22.6	15.4	-13.3	-29.7
Haiti	-2.8	-1.7	0.4	1.0
Cuba	143.6	321.4	33.4	163.6
Total	**5943.0**	**6334.4**	**6325.8**	**11486.1**
Latin America as % of developing countries[2]	29.7	32.0	21.2	24.4

Source: *Development Co-operation*, 1979 Review, OECD

1. a) Development Assistance Committee (DAC) countries: Australia, Austria, Belgium, Canada, Denmark, Finland, France, Germany, Italy, Japan, Netherlands, New Zealand, Norway, Sweden, Switzerland, United Kingdom, United States.
   b) Official Development Assistance (ODA) includes all bilateral and multilateral assistance but excludes aid from centrally planned economies.
   c) Total Recorded Net Flow of Resources comprises the following categories:
   i. Official development assistance
   ii. Other official flows
   iii. Grants by private voluntary agencies
   iv. Private flows at market terms (including direct investment)
   Categories i. and ii. are excluded from the figures in Table 1 and bank lending is included only insofar as reported by DAC Members.
2. Developing countries as defined in Note 2 of Table 1. Appendix 1.

Outward Direct Net Investment by Country (excluding oil) 1970-1976
(Net investment includes unremitted profits)

£ million	1970	1971	1972	1973	1974	1975	1976
Argentina	-0.3	-2.1	7.8	2.6	6.1	8.7	18.5
Brazil	12.1	11.3	21.0	34.1	34.2	60.6	67.2
Chile	0.3	0.6	-1.6	-0.1	0.6	0.4	0.7
Colombia						1.4	2.5
Mexico	-1.3	9.9	3.3	-5.8	3.1	6.6	2.1
Panama	0.1	. .	1.3	0.8	3.4	-0.3	-2.1
Peru	-0.3	0.5	-0.3	–	–	1.1	0.2
Uruguay	-0.3	. .	–	0.2	-0.2	. .	0.2
Venezuela	0.1	-0.2	0.7	-0.1	–	1.8	0.6
'Other'[1]	-8.3	-2.7	3.5	8.0	8.7	-18.7	40.7
Latin America as % of developing countries[2]	10%	25%	35%	15%	20%	25%	20%

Source: *Overseas Transactions 1976*, Department of Industry, Business Statistics Office, HMSO 1978

1. Other Non-Commonwealth countries in the Caribbean, Central and South America
2. Some investment figures are not available (indicated by the symbol . .) and the 'other' category (see note 1) is not clearly identified as comprising Latin American countries only. The percentages are therefore approximations.

Table 3: Stock of Direct Investment in Selected Latin American Countries by Country of Origin, Selected Years

	Argentina 1973	Brazil 1971	Brazil 1976	Colombia 1971	Colombia 1975	Mexico 1971	Mexico 1975	Panama 1969	Panama 1974
Total value of stock (US$ million)	2274	2911	9005	503	632	2997	4736	214	534
Distribution of stock (percentage)									
United States	39.5	37.7	32.2	55.9	48.1	80.9	68.7	90.8	86.3
Canada	3.9	10.1	5.3	10.1	10.1	1.7	2.3	–	–
EEC Countries	32.4	27.6	24.2	10.8	12.5	10.2	11.7	2.6	3.2
Other Western Europe	11.5	8.6	13.3	2.8	4.6	4.8	4.2	2.5	2.3
Japan	0.3	4.3	11.2	0.1	0.6	0.7	1.3	–	–
Latin America	3.9	3.2	3.4	9.3	11.6	0.2	2.5	–	–
Other Countries	8.2	8.7	10.4	13.0	12.5	1.7	9.3	4.0	8.1

Source: *Transnational Corporations in World Development: A Re-examination*, UN, New York 1978

Appendix 3 – Aid

Table 1: Net Receipts by Latin American Countries of Bilateral and Multilateral Development Assistance from DAC Countries[1], 1975-1978

	Income Class[2]	1975 B'lat	1975 M'lat	1976 B'lat	1976 M'lat	1977 B'lat	1977 M'lat	1978 B'lat	1978 M'lat
US$ million									

Argentina	UM	5.0	18.6	6.6	24.3	8.9	19.2	9.8	19.1
Uruguay	UM	1.4	11.2	2.9	9.9	2.1	5.9	2.2	7.9
Paraguay	LM	12.3	24.9	17.5	23.9	25.2	22.8	20.8	20.9
Brazil	UM	115.7	49.6	78.1	32.4	57.8	21.7	75.7	34.1
Bolivia	LM	32.2	24.4	45.7	21.0	57.6	35.8	85.6	59.6
Chile	UM	104.4	23.9	4.6	3.6	2.2	8.8	-14.0	21.9
Peru	LM	53.4	21.0	54.3	19.8	72.4	23.8	120.0	20.5
Ecuador	LM	25.4	45.0	37.2	38.6	22.9	31.9	23.5	19.0
Venezuela	H	1.2	17.5	-16.6	16.2	-10.4	10.4	-18.4	2.5
Colombia	LM	61.9	24.2	57.7	19.0	31.4	17.1	51.7	22.2
Mexico	UM	9.2	52.3	9.9	53.4	5.8	43.3	8.4	10.3
Panama	UM	20.1	13.1	27.4	14.6	22.9	12.1	18.7	10.1
Costa Rica	LM	17.3	13.3	11.7	12.8	14.5	10.2	34.1	16.6
Nicaragua	LM	18.4	23.0	18.6	20.6	18.7	17.7	26.5	15.6
Honduras	LM	28.1	24.5	23.0	17.1	22.9	34.1	33.9	58.2
El Salvador	LM	11.9	29.8	12.8	17.3	20.0	24.7	26.3	45.5
Guatemala	LM	26.9	13.1	43.7	21.6	37.2	24.6	26.3	45.5
Dominican Republic	LM	16.2	14.5	19.9	13.1	10.5	22.4	9.4	39.6
Haiti	L	24.8	34.5	32.1	39.6	39.6	46.8	49.8	39.9
Cuba	LM	14.3	6.7	26.0	9.9	29.7	15.5	17.4	21.7
Total		600.1	485.1	513.1	428.7	491.9	448.8	607.8	514.8
Latin America as % of developing countries[3]		6.1	12.6	5.4	11.1	4.9	9.0	4.6	8.7

Source: *Development Co-operation*, 1979 Review, OECD

1. Development Assistance Committee (DAC) Countries: Australia, Austria, Belgium, Canada, Denmark, Finland, France, Germany, Italy, Japan, Netherlands, New Zealand, Norway, Sweden, Switzerland, UK, USA.
2. L = Low Income Country (average per capita income in 1976 below approx. $400); LM = Lower-Middle Income Country (average per capita income in 1976 between approx $400-$1000); UM = Upper-Middle Income Country (average per capita income in 1976 between approx. $1000-$2500); H = Higher Income Country.
3. Developing Countries as previously defined.

Table 2: British Aid to Latin America: Public Expenditure on Overseas Aid. Gross Disbursements of Bilateral Aid, 1974-1978

£ thousands	1974	1975	1976	1977	1978
Argentina	124	124	61	24	15
Bolivia	353	376	620	1471	1062
Brazil	1850	3348	2263	1213	719
Chile	451	324	943	2073	1079
Colombia	902	2552	1312	1229	863
Costa Rica	849	4567	1645	777	462
Dominican Republic	29	25	39	53	107
Ecuador	718	1195	4838	2037	1795
El Salvador	286	753	316	308	413
Guatemala	-9	15	255	3	35
Haiti	6	35	38	20	6
Honduras	82	275	197	598	313
Mexico	406	733	633	847	828
Nicaragua	248	398	287	405	186
Panama	95	41	32	28	78
Paraguay	41	103	123	164	226
Peru	664	1610	1125	3570	820
Uruguay	28	24	43	39	27
Venezuela	112	48	7	6	4
Total	7235	16547	14777	14865	9039
Latin America as % of total gross disbursements of bilateral aid	2.7	5.4	3.9	3.8	1.7

Source: *British Aid Statistics 1974-78*, Ministry of Overseas Development, HMSO 1979

Table 3: Total Net Disbursements of Development Assistance from EEC Countries

US$ million		Bilateral Aid	Multilateral Aid
Austria	1977	86.5	31.3
	1978	112.8	53.0
Belgium	1977	261.9	109.1
	1978	310.4	225.7
Denmark	1977	147.1	110.8
	1978	217.3	170.3
France	1977	1916.9	349.9
	1978	2350.6	354.7
Germany	1977	1028.2	357.9
	1978	1560.7	857.7
Italy	1977	34.9	151.2
	1978	22.3	153.1
Netherlands	1977	643.6	256.0
	1978	789.2	284.3
UK	1977	555.4	358.8
	1978	852.5	619.9
Eire	1978	5.2	10.7

Source: *Development Co-operation*, 1979 Review, OECD

Appendix 4 – Arms Sales

Arms Sales to Latin America: Major Identified Arms Agreements, July 1978-June 1979

Recipient	Primary supplier	Date of agreement	Systems	Quantity	Cost ($m)	Expected delivery
Argentina	Austria	Late 1978	Kuerassier SP ATK guns	120	n.a.	n.a.
	France	Aug 1978	Puma hel	12	n.a.	n.a.
		Mid-1978	A69 frigates	2	n.a.	1979
		Mid-1978	SA-315 Lama hel	12	n.a.	n.a.
	Germany	July 1978	Frigates	6	900	1983
	Israel	Aug 1978	Mirage 5 fighters	26	200	1979
	USA	Mid-1978	KC-130 tanker ac	2	29.4	n.a.
			UH-1H utility hel	2	n.a.	n.a.
			King Air tpt ac	6	n.a.	n.a.
Bolivia	France	Mid-1978	SA-315B Lama hel	5	n.a.	Feb 1979
	Netherlands	July 1979	F-27 400m tpt ac	5	n.a.	1979
	Taiwan	Mar 1979	T-6 trg ac	10	n.a.	1979
Chile	USA	Mid-1978	Cessna Hawk trg ac	18	1.1	1979
Cuba	USSR	Mid-1978	F-class submarine	1	n.a.	Dec 1978
			Turya FAC(T)	2	n.a.	Dec 1978

Country	Supplier		Equipment			− Mar 1979
		Mid-1979				Oct 1978
						1979
Ecuador	France		MiG-23 *Flogger B*	20	n.a.	− Mar 1979
			W-class submarine	1	n.a.	Oct 1978
	France	Mar 1979	Sextuple *Exocet* SSM	6	n.a.	1979
	Italy	Oct 1978	650 ton corvettes	6	n.a.	n.a.
	USA	Early 1979	*Chaparral* SAM	18	n.a.	n.a.
			M-167 *Vulcan* towed 20mm AA guns	28	n.a.	n.a.
			M-163 *Vulcan* 20mm SP AA guns	44	n.a.	n.a.
Paraguay	Brazil	April 1979	EMB-326 *Xavante* ac	12	12	1979
Peru	Netherlands	Mid-1978	*Holland* class destroyers	2	n.a.	1979

Source: *The Military Balance, 1979-80,* International Institute for Strategic Studies, 1979

Abbreviations:

AA — anti-aircraft
ac — aircraft
ATK — anti-tank
FAC(T) — fast attack craft (torpedo)
hel — helicopter(s)

SAM — surface-to-air missile(s)
SP — self-propelled
SSM — surface-to-surface missile(s)
tpt — transport
trg — training